Sticky Buns Across America

Back-roads biking from sea to shining sea

Léo Woodland

McGann Publishing
Cherokee Village, Arkansas

Published by McGann Publishing
P.O. Box 576
Cherokee Village, AR 72525
USA
www.mcgannpublishing.com

McGann
Publishing

ISBN 978-0-9859636-0-6
Printed in the United States of America

To Jim Couch, a true friend when we needed one.

The test of an adventure is that, when you're in the middle of it, you say to yourself, "Oh, now I've got myself into an awful mess; I wish I were sitting quietly at home." And the sign that something's wrong with you is when you sit quietly at home wishing you were out having lots of adventure.

—*Thornton Wilder*

Prologue

Life is not a journey to the grave with the intention of arriving safely in a pretty and well-preserved body, but rather to skid in broadside, thoroughly used up, totally worn out, and loudly proclaiming "Wow! What a ride!"

Sid Saltmarsh was a tall, cadaverous man with a mustache like underarm hair. He had the air of being nicotine-stained well beyond his fingers. Some form of rot had set in uncontrollably. Nothing about him ran in straight lines. What might reasonably be straight was crooked. Or stretched and baggy. His collars had the shape of the cigarette ends in the saucer on his desk. His trousers were too short and too large.

You didn't need to examine Sid to know there was a soup stain somewhere.

Sid was the salt of the earth. I never did find out his age but to me, barely 20, he'd lived for ever. He'd been cycling correspondent of the *Daily Herald* when men still rode black Raleighs with celluloid mudguards to watch the cycling at Herne Hill. There wasn't much cycling on the radio then and word had it that Sid lost what little freelancing there was from the BBC when a break in the cricket forced the studio to go over to Herne Hill. At just that moment there was a similar lull in the cycling. Radio audiences were generous in the 1950s, but only in number. They weren't generous in the sense of being forgiving and nobody can be sure how many millions heard Sid's polished words: "Oh fuck, not now!"

Léo Woodland

Sid was deputy editor of *Cycling* in a cubby hole of an office so buried in the corridors of the International Publishing Corporation above the Golden Egg in Fleet Street that our policy was never to mention we were there. *Cycling* the magazine had gone through as hard a time as cycling the sport, and an editor doing his best had even taken on the then-exciting new mopeds, an expansion which succeeded only in driving away half the remaining readers. Its bosses in the past had included an imperious gent called H.H. England, who traveled first class to the printer's and waved to his staff back in third class as he made his way to the bar.

The editor in Sid's day was Alan Gayfer, a frog-like East Londoner and boxing enthusiast short enough to sit sideways on his chair with his feet in a drawer and touch-type. Most journalists peck with two fingers and neither know nor care what's going on around them. In Sid's case there was little chance of seeing anyway because the pile of old papers, race programs and notes rose round three sides of his desk and kept him safe from nuclear war if not a second Fire of London.

It was this lack of order which every few years comfortingly denied him any chance of becoming Liberal representative for the London suburb of Dulwich. He stood repeatedly for the council, for parliament, for anything, knowing he would never be elected. The Liberals were Britain's third party. Then came a change in fortunes and their leader, a boyish man called David Steel, told his members to "go home and prepare for government." No man was more worried than Sid.

Gayfer, powerful enough to demand that Sid rise now and then above his papers, and aware of his staff's shortcomings by being able to look around as he typed, rid *Cycling* of both its mopeds and of a steady procession of writers. But not Sid. Sid was bombproof. The two argued regularly and Sid would sulk, but Gayfer respected Sid "because Sid's an old newspaper man."

And that was how Sid came to tell me of the Unknown Cyclist. He was a figure he wished he could help when, cruelly for a man not much fond of humanity before lunch, he was sent early each Monday to *Cycling's* printers in Bournemouth.

"What we need, boy," he would snort or cough or growl, "is what they had on the *Evening News.*" The London *Evening News* was among an impressive list of failed newspapers on Sid's résumé. The reason we at *Cycling* kept so quiet about our existence is that we believed only IPC's oversight meant *Cycling* hadn't yet joined them.

"You know when a page is made up by the printers?" he asked, old sage to mere apprentice. I said I did, though I hadn't seen it because I'd never been exposed to one of Sid's trips to the world of Linotype machines and clickers and fathers of the chapel. "Then you know sometimes there's a hole where there's not quite enough type and it's too much trouble for the printer to space it out to fit?" He was referring to the pre-computer days of sliding slivers of lead between each line of a story to stretch it across the space the text-editor had designed for it.

"Well," said Sid, "there was this printer at the *Evening News* who used to carry an inch of story in his pocket, with the lead all wrapped round with an elastic band to keep it together. He had it ready for emergencies, see? And when he found a hole, he'd slip in this inch of type to fill it and when they'd printed the paper he'd pull it out again and wipe off the ink and save it for next time."

"And what did it say?" I asked.

"'It said 'An unknown cyclist was knocked down this morning as he rode over Waterloo Bridge. He was not seriously hurt.' Always used to appear, early editions, before the news room could come up with anything to fill the space. Saved delaying the page, see? You look up and see how often that story used to get in the paper somewhere." Now, I've no idea whether this was a libel on the printers of the *Evening News* but it did seem a useful idea. Unknown cyclists were indeed always being knocked down but not seriously hurt on Waterloo Bridge. Or, if they weren't, nobody was surprised to hear that one had been.

"What we need on this paper, Gayfer," Sid demanded not for the first time as he returned from Bournemouth and settled behind the trench fortifications of his paperwork, "is a stick of copy like that. Very useful."

A stick...

Journalists and printers in those days lived their own lives of secret words and measurements. An em was a twelfth of an inch, but it could be more or less than that depending on how big the type was. There were slugs and standfirsts and hanging indents. All, the em aside perhaps, were reasonably consistent. But a stick was as long as you wanted. Some said it was probably four inches, but it could be more. Perhaps a lot less. Others said they'd settle for five inches. In any event, it was some handy sort of length that suited the purpose, something that filled a gap, enough for a little story but nothing very useful.

Léo Woodland

My life ever since has been devoted to little stories that rarely turn out very useful. This may turn out to be one of them. It's not, by the way, a cycling story. I had to travel somehow; a bike is how I chose to do it, because people talk to cyclists. As Ernest Hemingway said: "It is by riding a bicycle that you learn the contours of a country best, since you have to sweat up the hills and coast down them. Thus you remember them as they actually are, while in a motor car only a high hill impresses you, and you have no such accurate remembrance of country you have driven through as you gain by riding a bicycle."

I chose to ride across America, which has two clear sides. One is the Atlantic and the other the Pacific. If you talk specifically about the USA, it has Canada to the top and Mexico to the bottom. It is a square with two wet edges. Australia has sea all round it and you wouldn't know where to start. Europe has a west but no east. It drizzles into Asia.

The other good thing about America is that history started on one side and rode a horse to the other. It began in Williamsburg, where English colonists survived longer than those who'd tried before. They bobbed into Chesapeake Bay on the *Susan Constant, Godspeed* and the *Discovery* and set up home in woods and among puzzling birds and curious locals. That was April 1607. Two weeks later, 200 Indians pounced on them and killed two and wounded ten.

The settlement is huge in American history. It makes barely a mention in British schools. In Williamsburg, nothing bigger has ever happened and the town has lived on it ever since. I rode there four years ago to start my first bike trip across America. A huge row was going on elsewhere about whether a later wave of immigrants should be allowed to sing the national anthem in Spanish. *USA Today* said the national anthem in Spanish made 69 percent of Americans hot under the collar. Those who thought it OK, ranging from approving to indifference, came to 29 percent. Among the less impartial was George W. Bush, the president, who said: "People who want to be a citizen of this country ought to learn English, and they ought to learn to sing the national anthem in English."

Given his own way of speaking English, this encouraged surprise in many.

I spent three days riding to Williamsburg from the airport outside the nation's capital. On the way I stopped in Fredericksburg, another town trading on its history. A baldheaded man in the printing ink business shook his head over his paper and despaired of his leader.

"How can man like that go round the world lecturing other people on the way to live," he asked, of me and anybody who cared to listen, "when he hasn't seen any of it himself? We have a president who hadn't even been abroad before he was elected. So when he gets anywhere foreign and the local leader says to him 'What have you seen of our fine country, Mr President?', the most he can say is that he's had a good look at the road from the airport."

Few people think warmly of politicians but Americans talk about them, often with vitriol, whenever they can. In the 1970s I was trapped on a North Sea ferry with four young and very earnest Americans, with nowhere to escape their insistence that I have a view on Jimmy Carter. And that view, they wanted to hear. I said repeatedly that I didn't have a view. He wasn't my president; he was a foreign politician, significant, but making little difference to my everyday life. When they pressed hard, I told them he smiled a lot and you could never think hard of a man for doing that. Their despair was obvious. They wanted to hear he was ruining the country.

Moments later they thought I must at least have a view on events in Britain, where everyone was on strike at the time, the fire brigade would no longer come to your burning house, and dead bodies and rubbish bags were piling up in the street. Again, I couldn't help. I lived in Belgium, I told them. That was why I was on the ferry from Zeebrugge. I could tell them about tram strikes in Antwerp and coal mines in Charleroi. I knew Stella Artois was excellent for cleaning your car but not to be trusted as a beer. I tried irony and said: "Well, at least the bread lines are getting shorter."

I should have seen my mistake.

"Gee," one of them said, "will there be food to eat? We'd heard things were bad but we had no idea they were that bad."

The man I met riding into Williamsburg was altogether lighter. He rode over with a little rearview mirror on his helmet as I tried to work out the streets from my map.

"Need help?"

"Think I do," I agreed.

He spotted my accent.

"Hey, a foreigner, huh?"

"No," I said straight-faced, remembering my British origins. "A former owner."

"And you're back now to see how we've coping since you been gone, right? Please don't be too critical."

For a moment the conversation faltered as his eyes changed focus. He was looking in his mirror. Behind him was a slender *chiquita* who'd turn any man's head. Except that my friend hadn't needed to turn his.

"You're a dirty old man," I chided with a laugh.

"Yeah, but I'm a dirty old man who got a better look at her than you did. Close to useless in traffic, mirrors, but when it comes to eyeing up women without their knowing, there's nothing better. That's the only reason I keep it."

I asked him what there was in Williamsburg.

"Wonderful place," he said with genuine pride. "The whole downtown's restored just as it was. You'll see. You could spend three days here, really. Course, it's all relative. I'm American and to me this is all really old. But my family, they're Greek. Imagine what *they* make of American history. 17th century? Don't make us laugh!"

He chuckled, slapped me on the back, urged me to get a mirror to look at attractive women, then rode off into town.

That ride across America ended in a mountain of medical bills in flat Kansas. I'd call it a saddle boil had there been any infection. But there wasn't. Just a swelling as thick as and half the length of my little finger. I shipped my bike home from Hutchinson and flew to France on an expensive one-way ticket. The nearest airport to Kansas appeared to be Chicago. I went by overnight train and loved it and the bike went in a box, looked after by one of those big shipping companies because I couldn't take it on the train.

Greed was my undoing. The shippers offered $1,000 insurance for no extra cost. For $2 I could have a further $1,000. I forget the precise figures but I do remember my cupidity as I worked out the odds of collecting, for just $2, around 20 times what the bike was worth. I signed up.

Why my undoing? Well, not because I paid $2 for nothing. It was because the box wasn't marked "personal effects." It was marked "bicycle." And Customs in France saw that, and the insured value of $2,000, and charged me import tax accordingly. How can you get out of that? Who had said it was worth $2,000? And if it hadn't been $2,000, why insure it for that much? The pain lives on.

Sticky Buns Across America

It lives on, too, from my second attempt. I planned to get to Seattle and didn't get to lunch. Two hours into the first morning I fell on one of the many potholes, uneven patches and ridges that are Boston's roads. I got up, walked about a bit, winced to the point of tears when I got back on my bike, and rode another 10 miles. After a while, I sat by the roadside for a banana. And I couldn't get up. Three cyclists called an ambulance. At the hospital they took an X-ray and, on its edge, noticed "a little dent". A second scan showed I'd broken my pelvis. I flew home business class with a wheelchair waiting in Paris and an ambulance in Toulouse. It wasn't the best way to spend a weekend in Boston but at least I didn't pay tax on my own bike.

MAY

America is a large, friendly dog in a very small room. Every time it wags its tail, it knocks over a chair.

—*Arnold Toynbee*

1

You guys nuts or summ'n?

Every journey should have a purpose, a cultural purity. There's so much to look forward to: the magnificence of Niagara Falls, the majesty of the Rockies, the chance of bumping into Pamela Anderson. But North America has, too, the Dan Quayle Vice-Presidential Museum, the world's largest boot, a display of outdoor privies, and a bank with an otter in a tank. I want to see where Charles de Gaulle waved his enormous arms at a crowd and boomed "*Vive le Québec! Vive le Québec... LIBRE!*", occasioning a speedy retreat from Canada with barely the hint of a blush. I want to see where oil first came gushing commercially from the earth, setting off the modern world. I want to go into a nuclear missile bunker, look round the Boeing factory near Seattle, see Judy Garland's childhood home. I want to see where the Sundance Kid robbed a train. And above all, I want to eat Sticky Buns.

I've told many of my adventures to the patient Mrs. Woodland. She has listened without comment, moving her lips with mine as I tell her the same story yet another time. I have told her of American Sticky Buns, the pleasure of sitting at a Formica table beneath neon lighting and peeling the wrapping off a gas station bun. And despite that, she wants to come as well. What's more, she wants to go further. She wants to see the Canadian as well as the American Rockies. She wants to see the Icefield Parkway, inspired as I was by pictures of her mother's train trip through the mountains.

And so we shall ride from Montreal—because it's easy to get to and because British Airways takes bikes with no trouble and little cost. We shall ride south of the Great Lakes and across to the Mississippi, there turning to the Canadian border. We'll follow the border with excursions to the north until we reach the Pacific, an ocean the patient Mrs. Woodland has seen but I never have. Seattle, I'm assured, is barely visible for all the hula girls dancing in straw skirts and little else.

Then north again, on through Vancouver, through the glacier fields and round to Calgary, chosen again because that's where planes go from. If they lose the bikes on the way back from there, I won't care. Now they're insured for their proper value. And if they turn up late at Toulouse, the airline will deliver them to us at home. So much more convenient than carrying them yourself, don't you think?

Losing them at Montreal, however, wasn't something we'd planned. And yet there they weren't: the empty carousel no longer turning, the baggage area no longer manned, the walls bare of bike boxes propped against them.

Would we ever see them again?

"Not more lost bikes," the dark-haired woman despaired at the baggage claims office.

"*More* lost bikes?"

"A load went astray this morning. A group arrived with only half their bikes."

"And my guitar," a lean man added with a Zen expression. Everything that was an unusual shape had disappeared. But where? Somewhere in Pierre Trudeau airport, in which case there was hope provided someone had the inclination to look? Or back in Heathrow, where we'd changed planes?

"If they're not here they'll come on the next plane," the woman said, switching between French and English.

"And that's…"

"Same time tomorrow."

We looked suitably glum.

"We'll bring them to your hotel, though," she promised. She gave us forms with which she could clear Customs with someone else's baggage and sent us across to the *Douanes* for a rubber stamp. And there, between the office and the empty carousel, stood our bikes. And the Zen man's guitar. We loaded the bikes but not the guitar into a taxi. The driver planned to change the world. He was in his 20s, round-faced, from Lebanon. He and his Moroccan wife had "fabricated a baby". He drove one-handed along concrete-walled roadways that merged and separated. It made sense on a map but the only progress was that the low, flat-topped buildings of the airport turned to high-rise blocks with international names in blue neon.

"I study by day and I drive a taxi at weekends," he said. "I've invented this software which will…" He went off in a dreamy explanation of turning primitive computers and internet connections into lion-sized operations to bring the modern world inexpensively to the African bush and Indian plain. I said I was impressed. I hadn't understood a word and didn't care to have it explained again.

"So I was going to e-mail the head man in the biggest computer companies in the world and tell them what I've created and start a panic. They'll all realize they absolutely have to have it, that they can't let it fall into the hands of the competition, and they'll start a bidding war."

I said it sounded a striking proposition. I had chosen my words carefully.

So had Charles de Gaulle. *Le grand Charlot* was brought up by Jesuits. He became so accustomed to learning long passages at their insistence that the habit stuck. He could address parliaments without notes and not vary a word from scripts given to journalists beforehand. His other talent was knowing he was right. Or, at any rate, believing the world was wrong. There's no doubt he knew what he was doing when he stood on the balcony of Montreal's city hall.

It was 1967 and the liberation movement in Québec had been planting bombs for three years in the cause of separation from English-speaking Canada to the west. The Québecois, lacking so dominant a symbol of their own Frenchness, flocked to de Gaulle. He'd been visiting Expo 67, a world's fair that drew more than 50 million visitors to the city. Going to the 19th-century Hôtel de Ville—the city hall—was a formality at which he hadn't been scheduled to speak. When he relented, probably with little resistance, to the crowd's insistence that he address them, he said his drive down the St. Lawrence, lined with cheering crowds, reminded him of Paris after liberation. He spoke of Montreal's progress in the modern world and concluded with "*Vive Montréal ! Vive le Québec!*"

But then he added "*Vive le Québec libre!*" The crowd was emotional. Federalists were outraged. He had called for Québec to secede. He was sent home. He said privately beforehand: "I will hit hard. Hell will happen, but it has to be done. It's the last occasion to repent for France's cowardice." He was referring to how France had abandoned 60,000 French colonists to the British in the war of 1763. He had a long memory, *le grand Charlot.*

The Hôtel de Ville was quiet when we walked past. Places often look smaller than their significance and Montreal's city hall was no exception. Some was that it was shrouded for work on the facade. De Gaulle's balcony was clear enough but there were no crowds, no waving blue and white flags. And—decide for yourself if this is odd or not—no historical marker remembering July 24, 1967.

There were, though, thousands of locals in shorts and minis, turning slowly red in the sun. It was May 2, "the first warm day we've had all year," a shopkeeper told us, "and everybody's desperate to make the most of it before it ends." And it did end. Next morning we set off in rain, riding past two prostitutes in bra, panties and backless dresses who were bickering over a public phone box. At 8am.

Our way south towards the border took us beside the traffic on the long, gray and wet Jacques-Cartier bridge across the St. Lawrence. It's just short of three and a half kilometers long and, according to the tourist office in the city, the fenced bike paths on each side don't exist. They do, though, and they're part of the city's admirable deal which includes bikes rented by the hour or the day from racks on the street, parking meters which have lock rings for bikes, and bike paths on most of the principal streets.

Québec, of course, was French and remains French by character if not nationality. The fact that France found it when it wanted to find China is only as comical as Columbus finding America when he thought he'd reached India. Things were like that in those days. Invaders are not quick to learn the language of where they arrived and the French, like English settlers further south, imposed their own way of talking. The one exception is the name Québec, itself. That is Algonquin, *kébec* being a narrow stretch of water. Curiously, that's also what *détroit* means, but the French saved that for further south.

(Come inside these brackets for a moment and I'll tell you that the founder of Detroit came from a village near here in France. His name was Antoine de La Mothe Cadillac and Cadillac cars are named after him. They should have been called Laumet cars, because that was his name. Like many a man, Antoine Laumet wanted to impress a woman. He moved to North America, where his father had fled to escape a legal bill, and adopted his far more impressive name, including the *de la* which implies nobility. The village of St-Nicolas-de-la-Grave, between Toulouse and Bordeaux, holds a Cadillac rally each July 14, the French national holiday.)

Québec stayed part of France for two centuries, whereupon the British arrived and the French, at the point of a bayonet but understanding the value of Caribbean sugar, traded it for Guadeloupe. That's why, if you look at a euro note, there's a tiny outline of Guadeloupe in the corner. Guadeloupe is part of France and it uses the euro.

There's no hiding Québec's heritage, though. Its language is French. All but five percent of the population speaks French and English is not officially recognized, although it can be used in courts. To my ears, the accent sounds harsh. It has pronunciations and expressions that have died out in mainland France. The differences are greater than between American and European English. I don't like the accent but native French speakers—I'm French by naturalization, not by birth— find it appealing. Among the most appealing is the use of *dépanneur* to mean a small store that stocks everything. In metropolitan French a *dépanneur* is a breakdown truck. Both truck and shop help you in a fix.

Montreal is appealing in the center, although not old, but the housing areas are like anywhere else. The outer belt is equally dreadful, a moonscape of steel huts selling car tires, fast food, motorbikes and carpets. Not finding the Route Verte bike path condemned us to spend a morning negotiating this Shedland of secondary businesses. And it was then that we stopped at a *dépanneur* for a lighter. Airlines allow neither gas canisters nor lighters and we needed to cook.

"*Vous cherchez?*" the woman behind the counter asked.

We told her we wanted a *briquet*.

"*C'est quoi, un briquet?*"

She didn't know the word. How could she not know what a briquet was? She sold dozens a day to smokers. We mimed lighting a cigarette and said we needed it for our *réchaud*, our stove.

"*Ah, un lighter!*"

We told the story to Gilles du Temple. He smiled. Like many educated Québecois, he is bilingual. He could see the joke. He also saw us when we didn't see him, because he'd turned and followed us to the post office in Chambly, where Montreal stops being Montreal. It's also where France was determined to keep Québec French. The lake that runs from Chambly into the USA is named after Samuel de Champlain, the first European to see it. He wrote: "The approach to the rapids is a sort of lake into which the water flows down, and it is about three leagues in circumference. Near by are meadows where no Indians live, by reason of the wars. At the rapids there is very little water, but it flows with great swiftness, and there are many rocks and boulders, so that the Indians cannot go up by water; but on the way back they run them very nicely. All this region is very level and full of forests, vines and butternut trees. No Christian has ever visited this land and we had all the misery of the world trying to paddle the river upstream."

"Where are you from? Where are you going? I ride a bike as well. Have you got time for a coffee?", Gilles enthused. His abundant gray hair was parted on the left. His mustache was a little darker and his eyes twinkled behind glasses. He wore a blue sports shirt and slacks. He led us past the substantial fort at a pace that wouldn't have been bettered by the original soldiers. He had become our appointed guide.

"This is a strategic point," he explained. The river churned and raced behind railings. A rising southerly wind stretched the maple leaf flag on its post. "You have to remember that the French controlled Canada and that they feared attack from the south. Anyone who passed this point would have free access to the St. Lawrence and therefore to everywhere beyond." We asked what being Québecois meant to him. He said it was his heritage. He spoke French, he spoke English, he was Canadian but he was from Québec. I said I'd noticed car license plates had the legend *Je me souviens*—I remember. But *what* do they remember?

"It means…" He paused and laughed. "Well, to be honest, I don't rightly know what it means." There is enjoyable irony in boasting you remember only to forget what it was you remembered. It turns out nobody knows. Someone ordered it to be engraved beneath a coat of arms on the provincial parliament but never said what he had in mind.

America and the state of New York arrived together at Rouses Point. The flat, open and muddy farmland of Canada sprouted an occasional red and white flag beside buildings as their owners tried to make a point. And then came the border crossing with its cameras, barriers and tire-shredding car immobilizers.

It costs a lot to go to the USA for more than three months. That's the limit without a visa: 90 days. To be honest, it costs a lot to go anywhere for longer than three months and it was with resignation that we'd paid $15 to get through to the US embassy web site, a further $140 for the visa, and then the train fare to Paris and an overnight stay to be inspected for suitability as tourists. Such things are normal in the world of international travel. What is less normal is to be charged a further $6 to get into the country. You buy a ticket for the USA as you would at a movie theater. You get a lot of country for $6, it's true, but why bother? Why not add it to the price of the visa? If you arrive by plane, the $6 is part of your fare, so why make the country look cheap by asking for small change at land borders?

There were two guards on duty, a smiling man in his 40s who sat in a white box and opened the barrier, and a younger, bright-eyed man who pecked at a computer with two fingers in the two-room building beside the gate. "*Higher dawn*," the older man asked said. "Where you guys headed faaah, anyway?" For the first time we fished out the small map we had printed for such moments. He traced the blue line across the US and then back up into Canada.

"Geez alive," he said. "You guys nuts or summ'n?"

He led us to his colleague to be fingerprinted, photographed and relieved of $6. "Y'know what these two ah doin'?" he shouted. He'd grown into shouting from yelling at drivers from his sentry box. The younger one made appropriate noises, dealt with us charmingly, then told us entry into America depended on asking his colleague how the Boston Red Sox were doing.

"Why?"

"He comes from Boston."

"And?"

"The Red Sox keep losing."

Things changed from that point. Until then we had been in featureless farmland and occasional villages so clinging to their existence that you wondered if they were long for this world. The moment we crossed into America was like the day you first saw color television. Rouses Point has never been a gem of sophistication but after rain-sodden Québec the lack of taste was welcome. The first thing after the New York sign, for instance, is the Git'n'Go Discount Duty Free store. Its sign is red, white and blue. The words "duty free" are larger than the words "New York" on the boundary sign. "Save up to 66%" the sign screams in diagonal red capitals.

Wow! America has arrived!

Rouses Point attracts more dollars than taste. It runs several miles along the main highway, a linear museum of kitsch in which houses are fronted by plastic swans, black jockey boys with thick, pale lips, and smug gnomes fishing in damp grass. Gangsters smuggled drink south across the border here during Prohibition. The village had a speakeasy called the Bucket of Blood. That good taste obviously prevailed.

The best story, though, shows again how the USA thinks the world is plotting against it. So many Canadians helped America get rid of the British that Rouses Point was given to them as a reward. That didn't stop America worrying that peaceful, dozy Canadians would rise up and attack it. And so it built a fort to keep them out. Sadly, they built it in the wrong place. Work was well advanced when someone pointed out they were inside Canada. This wasn't the way to good neighborly relations and so the Americans fled, leaving their half-finished fort behind them. The Canadians, who had watched with puzzled interest but with little intention to invade, took the stone and fittings to extend their own houses. It took three decades to realign the border so that the fort, or what was left of it, stood just inside America. It became known as Fort Blunder.

Ironville is the birthplace of the electric age in the United States. A white sign tells you so as you ride into the village. We hadn't intended to go that way but it made a short cut around Ticonderoga. And there, black italics on white plastic lookalike wood—we were already learning that little in the United States is what it looks like if there is a cheaper way of doing it—was the village's boast.

The only Ironville I knew was in the Derbyshire region of central England. There, the Butterley company built a model village, by which I mean not a miniature but housing of which its workers could previously only dream. Butterley made iron. Look at Vauxhall bridge over the Thames in London and you're looking at Butterley's work. But it's a big step from that to a tiny place with a big boast in upstate New York.

Well, yes and no. Iron was produced in Ironville, New York, as well. More precisely, ore was dug up in the neighboring hamlet of Hammondville and brought to Ironville to be separated. I suppose they grew tired of doing it by hand, or horse, or wind power or whatever they used and they—Allen Penfield, Timothy Taft and Allen Harwood, according to a separate sign—hit on plugging into the electricity supply. It was, the sign says, the first industrial use of electricity in the world.

Tom Davenport, the long-faced blacksmith in Brandon across the water in Vermont, went further and bought the electromagnet. In 1883 he made the world's first electric motor. What did he use it for? To run a little model car. Very American, don't you think?

We didn't have a car, nor an electric motor. We traveled with loads on our bikes, two bags on the back of Steph's and four on mine, two at the front and two at the back, plus our tent rolled above the back wheel. This first week was a challenge. Steph had shingles this past winter and barely rode her bike. In our first week, she rode further than all year. The first day's ride, out of Montreal, was further than any ride this year.

"I'm not worried about the distance," she kept saying. "I'm not worried about getting across America. I'm just worried about the first week."

Why? Because the first week crossed the Adirondacks, the northernmost end of the mountain chain known further south as the Appalachians. They never get high—around 1,000 meters on the road—but the climbs are long if neither lungs nor legs are ready. I struggled and Steph wilted. She faded. There are two ways to approach a long ride: one is to be fit before you start and the other is to get fit during the ride. The first takes time and the second inflicts pain. Steph was feeling that pain.

"Give me some of your load," I insisted.

She wouldn't hear of it.

"Look, we bought an extra bag for cases like this. Get it out, put some of your stuff in it and strap it to my bag."

She hesitated, looked defeated but grateful, and began unbuckling her panniers. Out of them she extracted the long, blue bag that could be unrolled to carry food or anything unexpected. The extra load now slowed me and after a couple of hours I, too, struggled. Every rise became an effort. Every big rise a mountain. I lay in grass by the roadside, my heart a pneumatic drill. If this was how the ride was going to be, we were going to get fit the painful way or it was going to turn into a four-month misery.

What made things more serious is that we had an appointment on the other side of the mountains. We had to meet an old friend, Ed Pavelka, with whom I'd stayed in touch since 1980 when he was editor of *Velo-News* and I was his writer in Europe. Ed had booked a hotel and the date nestled in the only available date in his wife Joleen's schedule of study and nursing exams. We'd considered this before the ride. I had scoured the net for one-way van hires, a way of getting through the worst even if it meant sacrificing scenery I was sure would be breathtaking. There weren't many options. In fact there was just one. And we had ridden past it because it was still flat.

Luckily, angels came to our rescue. Angels from Maryland, further south, one of those states that Europeans have heard of but have no idea where they lie. The angels were Richard and Karla. I met them four years ago on my failed-bottom ride to Kansas. Richard was one of the group and Karla, who is as short as Richard is tall, popped up along the route to bring delight and sunshine. Richard, slender, silver-haired and growling, used to be an engineer. Karla used to be a spy. She says she wasn't, that she just worked for the American state department in odd places like Monrovia, but... well, that's what spies *would* say, isn't it? I think she used to lead enemy agents across misty bridges at midnight. Her job was to meet an anemic man in a raincoat and say "I am Black Rabbit. Are you Dancing Bear?" And then she would exchange one captured agent for another and walk back across the river knowing that Kalashnikovs were pointed at her back. She probably knew John Le Carré. Or, even more probably, she just organized daily life in a foreign legation and had none of this fun at all. Shame, really.

Sticky Buns Across America

Richard and Karla came with their tandem, Black Jack, and with a large car. They took turns riding with us while the other drove carrying our bags. It wasn't the way we'd hoped but as a way of getting through the Adirondacks, and especially of getting Steph through the Adirondacks when the temperature was little above freezing and the wind blew and the rain fell, it was a blessing. We didn't know then that there was worse to come and that the angelic Richard and Karla would again come to our rescue.

America: land of the brave, home of the simply relaxed

The Adirondacks are the USA's largest state park, larger than several national parks—Yosemite, for instance, is a national park—added together. They are 25,000 square kilometers of rounded mountains largely covered by pines. The roads had a melancholy beauty I have seen only once or twice in my life. The pines stood sad beside the road, their shoulders slumped, their arms curved in a permanent shrug. In summer they despair of the heat, in winter they tolerate the cold. On the distant hills they looked like slender, horny matchsticks planted into the clay-color soil, their foliage no more than puffs of weak cotton stuck to their sides. Close up, lining the road, they took two forms. Those immediately beside the road were macho cowpokes, their shrugging arms revealed now as waiting over their holsters. They played bluff with the trees across the road, permanently on the edge of a shoot-out.

Behind these trees were smaller pines, a finer green, more fragile in growth. Their arms were raised. They were the womenfolk, sheltering behind their men, proud of them but scared at what might happen. Their arms stood frozen permanently in alarm. It brought to mind the words of Roderick Frazier Nash, that "We cannot teach our children what is special about our history on freeways or in shopping malls.... Protecting the remnants of wild country left today is an action that defines our nation. Take away wilderness and you diminish the opportunity to be American."

The Adirondacks are new as mountains go and they're still pushing upwards. Nobody lived here for centuries and the region had no name. Indians avoided it and early settlers had little reason to come. A map in the mid-18th century calls it just "deer-hunting country", which sounds like the cartographer filling in embarrassing gaps in the way that others wrote "Here be monſters" where they thought Australia might be but couldn't be sure. Nobody went there, so why bother being more specific?

The love of mountains is only recent. Before the 19th century people thought them desolate and forbidding. It was writers like James Fenimore Cooper and Henry David Thoreau and Ralph Waldo Emerson who gave them the aura of spiritual renewal. They started a rush of tourists, hotels and stage coaches. A railway opened. By 1875 there were 200 hotels, some with several hundred rooms. Attitudes to the mountains had changed so much that measures had to be taken to stop the destruction. In 1884 a commission recommended a reserve "forever kept as wild forest lands" and the following year the Adirondack Forest Preserve was created. The name has changed but the state constitution still insists that "the lands of the State…shall be forever kept as wild forest lands. They shall not be leased, sold, or exchanged, nor shall the timber thereon be sold, removed or destroyed."

The Mohawk would have been surprised. They hadn't wanted anything to do with the forests and they were dismissive of their neighbors, the Algonquians, who went into the woods and ate berries and bark when times were hard. They called them *ratirontaks,* "people who eat trees." The name stuck.

People who settled here took refuge down in the valleys and their farms reverted to nature within a decade. It wasn't hard to create a state forest. There still aren't many people here now. We rode for an hour without passing a building or a driveway. There was no commercialism, just a clean, winding, climbing road bathed in the cold, damp oxygen of a vast pine forest. The state of New York is different from the city of New York. There is money in the city. Four of the five top zip codes for political donations are in Manhattan. Here in upstate New York, as we have learned to call it, recession has struck. There were grand houses and failed businesses. Gas stations have lost their pumps but kept their rotting canopies, their names fading in the winter cold. Fading, too, were the signs that said they were for sale. They all represented someone's lost dreams, perhaps their lost fortunes.

"This place is run by accountants in Albany," a woman told us, referring to the city. "They know about the city but not what we're going through here."

We began noticing blue signs urging us to call our legislator to save Moriah Shock. We thought it was someone destined for the electric chair. Poor Moriah had done something wrong in life but the community wanted a second chance. I asked the woman what it meant. She said Moriah wasn't a person but a place. A Shock was a particularly unpleasant sort of jail. The woman looked sad, a run-down Mrs.Tiggywinkle, or perhaps a retired and fussy librarian. Her glasses were on a string round her neck. She wore a long skirt in a swirling pattern that reminded me of a bed quilt. Her concern was less for the juvenile delinquents who were sent there to run around a lot and obey orders than for those who lived around about.

"The state governor wants to close it," she said. "Shame is that for the kids who pass through, it works. For the community, they get sent out to work in society, so we'll lose all that good work. But more than that, a lot of people work there and a lot of businesses depend on it. That's going to hit us hard if that closes."

I read the *Adirondack Daily Enterprise*, "the only daily newspaper published in the Adirondack Park." It told me the governor wanted to save the $9½ million a year he spent on the place. More than 100 employees would lose their job unless they moved elsewhere. And the most likely "elsewhere" was a medium-security prison an hour's drive away in Ray Brook.

The boot camp did stay open in the end. But for a while the 100 people there and the 300 others in the area whose living depended at least in part on supplying it, saw hard times ahead. This was all such a contrast to the tale told us outside a café in Newcomb, a little further down the road. It had a porch and a door and, beside it, a serving hatch for ice cream. The woman came bounding out with a coffee in each hand, apologized that she might have spilled some on us, then launched into her tale. She had been born in Newcomb, she said, and now she had returned to retire after 40 years in nursing in Syracuse. Like the prison employees, she too had been working for New York State. She occupied herself now with the village school. Newcomb has fewer than 500 people and 80 children attend class there. They had, she said, a budget of $5 million.

"Our kids are getting a $60,000 education and nobody seems to have noticed," she said with more pride than guilt. "The facilities are wonderful. We've even set ourselves up as an exchange agency to bring in kids from abroad, to give them experience and to give our own children wider contacts." The children come here from all over Europe, keeping up the roll numbers if only temporarily and discouraging bean-counters in New York from looking closer.

"This year we're getting Russian children for the first time. They all comment how the mountains here remind them of home." We passed the school a few minutes later and noticed a sign announcing an imminent budget meeting. We wondered if it was good or bad news. Meanwhile, *USA Today* was reporting: "The state has begun closing 41 parks and 14 historic sites as the budget crisis continues." Selfishly, we wondered what that would mean for camping in state parks as the ride went on.

The American willingness to talk, exemplified by the woman at Newcomb is impressive. Europeans talk but only after being prized open. Inside you may find a pearl but you may discover nothing, which makes you wonder if the effort is worth it. Americans, on the other hand, are floppy, tongue-slobbering pet dogs who yearn for company, affection and human ear-tickling. They love meeting people, being friendly, and above all talking. Everyone is worth a few minutes, to see if he has a tale to tell.

Quentin Crisp, the naked civil servant who loved America so much that he moved here, wrote: "Everyone is eager. This is to me by far the most important attribute of Americans. They want to speak, they want to listen and they will endure quite a lot of inconvenience to prevent the color being drained out of experience. They like people to be unusual in any way they know how. Even being foreign will do. Visiting Englishmen they adopt as pets and coo at them as though they were budgies than can nearly speak American."

I once got talking about the Civil War at a gas station. Gas stations are all that remain of shops in much of rural America, offering not just petrol but a small supermarket and big jugs of coffee. Plus sticky and restorative buns. Ask a cyclist how he judges a civilization and he will cite the ability to supply buns. I mentioned to a man in blue dungarees and a checkered shirt that coffee was harder to come by in small garages in Europe but that for decades—until interference by hygiene inspectors—there had been a tradition in Britain of parking vans beside highways to serve tea, bacon rolls and cakes to anyone who cared to stop.

"It was tradition that a lot of these places flew a flag," I told my new friend. "Sometimes it'd be the skull and crossbones, the Jolly Roger, but as often as not it'd be the Confederate flag."

He asked why.

I said I didn't know. The Jolly Roger made sense in that these fly-by-night tea bars were outside the establishment, but the Confederate flag was a mystery. Either there was an association with the South breaking from the city mores of the North or, as likely, it reflected the taste for country music and line-dancing that seemed obligatory among the operators.

"Wouldn't do that here, any case," Dungaree Man said.

"What? Sell tea? Like country music?"

"No problem with tea, though coffee'd go down better. An' country music would be darned well obligatory in some parts. No, the

Léo Woodland

Confederate flag. You wouldn't do that here. It'd be taken as racist. The black folks'd say you was harping after slavery again.

"There are things you can discuss and things you can't. It's not easy, 'cause there are militants on both sides. You can't go pointing out that there weren't that many slaves here and you can't say they were sold into captivity by their own kind. It may be true but it doesn't pay to say so."

Inlet had just held its annual pizza-eating contest. The *Weekly Adirondack* reported at the top of page seven that "each contestant was required to tackle a medium-size with cheese. Max Cohen was able to eat his in just four minutes and 54 seconds."

Cohen, curly-haired with a long chin and indigestion, won $100 and another $100 in vouchers to buy more pizza. In the doubles competition Brian Caufield, in glasses and with his baseball cap backwards, and Chet Cohen, a bearded and curly-haired man in sunglasses who was no higher than his partner's ear and could have been related to Max (we weren't told), had to share just $50. It hardly seemed worth eating a large, two-topping pizza in three minutes and 36 seconds. But they looked happy enough.

Less happy was a fair-haired woman with the smile of a plastic doll. She wore a smart but forgettable dress, a cardigan and a small gold necklace. She was the wife of a retired army lawyer, she said, and she insisted that young French people hated "the military", by which she meant the French military. I told her I had no idea.

"You just ask them," she insisted, "any young person. They hate the military."

My first thought was that if she was right, it was because France persisted long after other nations in taking teenagers into national service. It took the oldest son and ended up with the less bright because boys at university didn't have to go. If those recruited showed no aptitude, they were marched up and down and made to polish boots. If they had talent as a racing cyclist, they joined the Joinville battalion and had the time of their lives. Soldiers called to Joinville include half the French champions of cycling history. Laurent Jalabert's recollection was that he did "nothing but ride a bike for two years."

I began to feel irritated. I could neither agree nor disagree, other than that the young are driven by ideals and against wars. It was more that I felt I was being pressed into an assumption that people *ought* to love soldiers, or have any feeling about them at all. Plus the implication that young people in America have nothing but affection for their armed forces, which I'm not sure is true. There was also my suspicion that she didn't speak French and therefore didn't know even as much as she could read in a newspaper. The idea that "any young person" hated soldiers could only have been hearsay.

It's true that American soldiers are fond of themselves—you see car plates inscribed "Retired US Army" or "Ex-Marine"—but that's not the same thing. Maybe this woman belonged to a circle where, being among people who saluted the flag, she felt herself more patriotic.

"The difference is that we do *still* have patriots here", she smiled, reveling in the assumption that the world and France in particular didn't. I could do nothing but shrug, smile and say good-bye.

When Americans got upset at the reluctance of other nations for a second invasion of Iraq, France for some reason got singled out for ire. At one level it was comical: menus in the three cafeterias of the Washington capitol building were changed from French Fries to Freedom Fries. "This action today is a small but symbolic effort to show the strong displeasure of many on Capitol Hill with the actions of our so-called ally," protested Bob Ney, whose part in foreign policy seemed limited to checking the knives and forks.

It fell flat in France. French people had never considered fries the slightest French; they'd always thought of them as Belgian. The same has gone for French vanilla, French silk cakes and French toast and French press coffee. All unknown in France. We began collecting rootless French references.

American rejection of France and the pouring of French wine down sewers just seemed ungrateful. "How quickly they forget La Fayette,'" my friend Laurence said in despair at the short-term view of history to which Americans seem doomed. And she had a point. This 23-year-old French nobleman, the Marquis de La Fayette—his title is shorter than his full name of Marie Joseph Paul Yves Roch Gilbert du Motier— offered his services to the American Revolution. And there he had risen to major-general, working for glory rather than money (he was unpaid), and closer to being Washington's war commander than many Americans are prepared to acknowledge. La Fayette brought in France to fight the mutual enemy, the British, and he brought almost all the gunpowder used by American troops. I wonder if anyone remembers him today. Outside France, that is.

The Adirondacks passed day by day, green, silent, beautiful, cold. Buffalo grazed in a valley, half beast, half man, the epitome of Ancient Greece where such things drew no comment. Why should they, when androgynous youths flew by on the backs of swans? The British elections passed without anyone knowing who had won. A man called Doug Fuegel grew heated about wind turbines: "Probably not since the knockdown, boisterous and sometimes violent Adirondack deer forums of the 50s and 60s have there been such loud and opinionated public meetings of recent concerning wind farms and their proposed locations," he wrote in a hunting magazine I picked up during a Sticky Bun Opportunity.

Turbines in the mountains? I hoped not. No, on lower ground, it seemed, and out on the Great Lakes. "If and when the Lake Ontario wind turbines become a reality in both New York and Canada, the total may reach more than four thousand turbines. Has any person or agency imagined the spectacle emitted at night with thousands upon thousands of red blinking lights all visible from shore along with the constant off-on day and night strobe lights?"

The Lakes were getting nearer. People were now talking of them. They—the lakes, not the people—were refilled by sleet-tinged rain that dropped on Old Forge, "destination for generations of visitors seeking everything from serenity to adventure." We had both. Richard and Karla found us a motel to hide from the deluge. And next morning it snowed. The serenity was broken by the scraping of snow and ice from windscreens, the spinning of tires in the car park. Could we ride? No, we couldn't. A coat of ice lay beneath the snow. On the road, things could be better. But who knew? Sometimes traffic cleared snow, at other times it compressed it into something unridable. We surrendered once more to Richard and Karla's generosity and let them drive us 40 kilometers down the road to Boonville, where we had that lunch date with Ed and Joleen Pavelka.

Ed was editor of *Velo-News* when it was a newborn back in the 1970s. I lived in Belgium and breathed the same air as Eddy Merckx, which was enough for Ed to recruit me as European correspondent. The only time we had met was in 1980, when a strange woman called K. K. Hall, her hair in a tight gray bun and her seemingly dead husband next to her in a scarlet pickup, organized a bike race for women from all over the world in the cactus hills around Tucson, Arizona. Among them was the then-current world champion, Josianne Bost. She doubtless found K.K.'s name amusing: K.K., pronounced *kah-hah* in French, is child speak for *merde*.

I don't know what happened to K.K. and Josianne. Ed, though, became editor of *Bicycling*, the world's largest cycling mag, before leaving in despair at its increasing fondness for mountain bikes in general and racing downhill in particular. Ed is a committed roadie with an impressive time in Paris–Brest–Paris, 1,200 kilometers which the leisurely ride in 90 hours and raging bulls like Ed achieve in markedly less. He thought it would be amusing if I rode with him. My part would be to cling to his wheel and see western France, there and then back, through tears. He considered it a genial way to cross the country. "But all you have to do is ride the qualifying distances this year and then again next year," he mused. Well, good gracious, viewed like that I see I'd have half the year to do almost nothing at all. Like a boss who tempts you to work 12 hours a day because you'd still have the other half of the day to yourself.

I said I couldn't because we were going to carry our home across Canada and the USA. Ed sees things like that as romantic but best left to others. Our friendship resumed the moment we met but Paris–Brest–Paris wasn't mentioned again. And probably won't be.

The most prominent building in Boonville is the "historic" Hulbert House hotel, built in 1812. It is stone with fussy white balconies built on white pillars that rise in front of the facade. Franklin D. Roosevelt and Buffalo Bill both stayed there. It probably seemed less rickety then. Now it had the air of a girls' boarding school. "The upstairs is for Overnight Guests ONLY!," warned a handwritten sign on the stairs. "NO LOITERING or you will be forced to leave!"

The lightness of touch extended to our room. "THERE IS TO BE NO SMOKING IN THE ROOMS. If caught you will be asked to leave & any damages will be charged to your account. Thank you. Hulbert House mgmt."

We saw signs that we were in a strange land. You don't, in Europe, see warnings that you're in a Drug-Free Zone. I found it sad that a community needed to say so. It could only have been wishful thinking since if drug-dealers and users chose to frequent the area, they'd hardly be put off by signs. Some were outside schools, which made the message even sharper. A few went as far as saying the zone extended to 150 yards of the school boundary. Never did I see any drugs, selling or using, but I am an old fart who wouldn't notice clues even if he saw them.

And what is it about Americans and trespass signs? There can be no nation more possessive of land than America. There is land and land and land, from here to the horizon, more land than any man might want. And yet every moment of it was fenced. And on the fences were signs marked POSTED which promised dreadful consequences for trespassing. Often there were many more signs than ever there were people. We could be out of sight of a house in all directions, on a road known only to passing birds and bees, and there would be these signs as though everyone feared a pop festival or a column of hippies would arrive at any moment.

But for all the land, rich or poor, there's no concept of gardening. Houses and shacks alike stood in open land, like Monopoly houses on a poker table. Not a hedge, natural or cultivated, still less a flower bed, broke the impression that half America wished it lived on a golf course. If lawn-cutting became an Olympic sport, America would excel. No nation is more in training. Barely a mile passed without yet another portly man in long shorts and mid-calf white socks (it's almost always a man, always long shorts, and never anything but ankle socks pulled to full height) driving a garden tractor as the cuttings shot everywhere. It is as close to bliss as an American comes.

On a bike, you carry only what you are prepared to pedal. Newton's law is reassuring: once you have the bike rolling, the weight of rider and bike and baggage make little difference. It's only when gravity gets involved that things turn nasty. For all their efficiency on the flat— twice the speed of running for a quarter of the energy—bicycles turn into wallowing sows on hills. The more you load them, the worse they get. So, while an athletic Italian in the Tour de France can notch the gear lever just once and cruise a mountain on the calorific power of an espresso, a touring cyclist finds himself pulling the gear lever like an old-fashioned signalman.

The benefit is that you travel at a human pace at the expense of one cup of coffee and a Sticky Bun every hour and a half. If you learn to take only what you need and you choose gears low enough, you can ride most mountains with less effort than you think and get slimmer, healthier and lighter in the process. That in turn makes the mountains even easier, although oddly it doesn't reduce the need for Sticky Buns.

At other end of the food chain comes the RV driver. Americans talk of RVs in a way that reduces the majestic, oceangoing foolhardiness of what they're talking about. A European, for whom a Recreational Vehicle could be little more than a moped, has trouble adjusting his eyes to the Panavision wide angle needed to take in the endless length of something so humbly named. RVs are not simply motor coaches stripped of seats and fitted with beds. They are intercontinental trucks fitted with every luxury and enough soft padding to contain even those crazy enough to buy one.

They are nature's way of showing you have too much money and a lack of proportion and shame. They are conspicuous consumption on wheels, literally true when you consider the petrol consumption. Nevertheless, people drive them on journeys that last months and folk have sold their houses to devote their lives to a five-star reconstruction of Jack Kerouac.

As if the length weren't enough, these road liners expand to create still more space. Big cubes of space emerge from their sides. It is like seeing a house give birth to a bungalow: a block the height of a room and as wide as many people's living rooms moves out of the body of the van and turns it into a crucifix. More than that, behind the RV is a trailer in matching colors and half the length. It is where the driver keeps his spare car. And a spare car he needs—usually one far larger than most people have for their first car—because the RV is too large to drive anywhere but interstates. The towed car is the rubber dinghy behind gin-palace yachts to get the owners into port, except that a dinghy is only a dinghy whereas the RV owner's ship-to-shore is often a four-wheel drive encrusted with chrome.

We saw RVs pulling not just cars but pickups. Pickups are the trophy of people who live in the suburbs and hope to encounter a dead moose outside Walmart. One or two pickups, driving all four wheels with engines as large as six liters, just may have been down a farm track or carried something more than shopping. But most are highway bragging.

Léo Woodland

The highlight of our day was to see an RV pulling a pickup which was itself loaded with a golf cart. We thought the owner was a golfer. But what would a golfer do with a pickup? It took a wiser mind to say that, no, the electric cart was to save walking round the RV park at night. You never knew what harm exercise might cause.

We had never come across a traffic roundabout in America and so I assumed Americans encountered them for the first time when they went to Europe. Near Mildenhall and Lakenheath, where England juts like an ear into the North Sea towards the rest of Europe, there were not only roundabouts on fast roads but a lot of servicemen fresh from America. Lakenheath is a fighter base and Mildenhall, a step away, is where American troops arrive before being sent on elsewhere in Europe.

American troops sent to Europe can take 10 tons of luggage and are allowed, although discouraged, to bring their own cars. If they do bring their own, they find themselves not only on the other side of the road but the wrong side of the car. If they buy a British car, they are both on the left of the road and the right of the car. It's not simple. The time came when one weary soldier approached a roundabout and, in a moment of blankness, went neither left nor right but straight up to the top of a high mound of grass. There his car balanced with none of the four wheels touching the ground. The American was rocking the car in the hope of inducing motion when he heard a police siren.

Accustomed to police back home, he turned towards his car, put his hands wide apart on the roof and spread his legs. And there he stood, waiting for an armed and no doubt cynical policeman to frisk and arrest him. Except that nothing happened. When eventually the driver looked round, it was to see a delighted and unarmed policeman surveying the scene with his hands on his hips and a look of amused exasperation on his face. And then in his roly-poly Suffolk accent, he said: "Well bless me, sir, I can't say as we see a lot of that round here."

It used to be, in New York as in other states, that motorcyclists had to wear helmets. In 1967, Washington bribed states to make them compulsory, saying they'd get no money for roads if they didn't. By 1975, 47 states had taken the money. But lobbyists complained that the law went against freedom of choice and in 1968 Michigan led in abandoning compulsion. The consequence in New York is that overweight Easyriders now roar about baldheaded, wearing red neck scarves, a look of unbearable superiority and the floppy mustaches you thought nobody had grown since 1976.

We were never convinced we'd need helmets in the snow because the roads, thankfully, were clear. Around us, though, beside the quiet, rolling roads that passed through mixed woods where the occasional animal rustled unseen, the previous day's fall lay beneath the trees. It was just two degrees above freezing but it was sunny.

I had been counting American flags. They run to hundreds a day. I have never been to a country with such passion for flying the flag, outside homes, outside public buildings and restaurants, outside shops and now, for heaven's sake, outside a rubbish tip. Fly the tricolor outside your house in France and it would be considered very odd. A nurse would ask if you felt all right. To fly the Union Jack in Britain hints you want India back. To fly the English flag—the red cross of St. George on a white background—has racist overtones unless there's a soccer match on. And even then British soccer was once notorious for racist chants and for bananas thrown at black players.

Out in the fields we passed a tall post with a Stars and Stripes floating languidly in the winter air. A larger than necessary sign advertised a rubbish tip. Now, what was that supposed to say? "Great American Rubbish"?

We were still pondering that when we passed a delightful graveyard behind a white fence just outside Redfield, snow lying in patches beneath trees which leaned over a variety of stones. It stretched only half the length of a soccer field. But there were 37 flags on the graves. So why?

"Because we do *still* have patriots here," the woman with views on French youth would have said. "Because it's what you do," Karla had said, speaking of flags outside houses. But these were dead Americans, no longer in a position to be patriotic. It wasn't a military cemetery and there was no national holiday celebrating the dead, former soldiers or not. It was just a graveyard. Steph went to count the flags while I looked from outside. We've noticed that some graveyards had flags and others not. It was all or nothing. Maybe someone plants a flag and others come by and get uppity and say: "Hey, honey, that dead guy's got a flag flying. We can't have people thinking our dead guy is less patriotic than their dead guy. Let's get a flag up there and quick." Now, America is nothing if not religious. The money is marked "In God we trust." There is no shortage of churches. Churchgoing in France is down to three percent. In America it is much, much more. So most people who buried their dead here believe that souls go from here to some superior kingdom. In which case, why fly the flag of a nation where the soul no longer lives and which, by acknowledgment, is nothing compared to the Kingdom of Heaven?

It would take an American to explain.

2

Oh gee, they sunbathe nood over there, don't they?

The first of the Lakes was now just half a day away: Ontario, in case your geography is weak. The land flattened and the villages were neither centers nor agricultural communities remote from anywhere. Redfield was an example. We rode in to find the food shop closed and the hotel burned down. Surrounding buildings were derelict. We tried the bar. The door was open but a busy, loud woman from the place next door rushed to tell us we couldn't go in. If we wanted to eat, there was a restaurant up the road.

"You go up there and say Cowgirl sent you," she urged. She had a weather-rendered face and a powerful voice.

"That's what they call you, Cowgirl?"

"It's what the locals call me. My name's Janna but I was always around cows and horses so they call me Cowgirl."

We rode on and found the restaurant, opposite a quiet road junction with a trailer parked in trees.

"Cowgirl said to be sure to say she sent us here," Steph said. It brought a blank look.

"She said her real name was Janna."

"Cowgirl? Pain-in-the-ass, you mean…"

Redfield is a village of 600 on the side of a reservoir that looked like a long, twinkling lake. Like almost everywhere in New York, it was dying. Decay was the theme everywhere we went; all that differed was the extent to which rot had set in. I put the idea to the restaurant woman but she didn't hear or acted as though she hadn't. She did acknowledge the hotel fire, though. It would have been hard not to, given the black wreckage on the main road.

"That was a big blow to Redfield when that burned," she said. "That was the biggest employer in town."

"Can you work here now?"

She shrugged. She had a job, she said. Her husband worked for the town's council and they lived in the trailer we'd seen across the road. "Most people here work in the wire factories. They commute to other towns round here."

"And the rest?"

"On farms, some of them." She didn't radiate hope or economic happiness. "We're managing OK."

One of many curious things that Margaret Thatcher said was that no two democracies had ever been to war with each other. She was wrong. On 13 Oct 1812 the US invaded Canada, taking advantage of Britain's back being turned while it fought Napoleon in Europe. The Royal Navy had been stopping US ships, saying it wanted to recover deserters but more probably to imprison American sailors and force them to fight on British ships. There were five Americans on HMS *Victory* at Trafalgar, along with French, Spanish, Dutch, Danish and Italian, and it seems few were there voluntarily.

War began with the USA on one side and Canada and Britain on the other. America should have done well. It had 7.5 million Americans and a regular army of 12,000. There were just half a million Canadians and fewer than 7,000 soldiers. Canada wasn't organized whereas America's frigates were powerful and had done well in an undeclared war with the French. The problem for the US was that it was poorly organized and that, the moment it moved against someone else, Indians at home rose against it.

I'm not going to recount the battles. The two things that interested us were that many of them had happened out here in the Great Lakes, as good a place as any to fight a naval battle with Canadians, and that they gave rise to the American anthem. We have never learned the words of the American anthem. We have never needed to. At school, we knew the most powerful lines of the *Marseillaise* (*Aux armes, citoyens!*) were or should have been *Où est le papier*, a tribute to shortcomings of French public lavatories, just as we knew the last lines of the American anthem were:

Sticky Buns Across America

So bring us figgy pudding
We all want figgy pudding
We love our figgy pud
So bring some today

Marseillaise is about rising up and leaving the impure blood of foreigners in the gutter before they "fall upon us and tear the guts from our sons and wives." That is what anthems should be like, not this nonsense about figgy pudding. When I finally heard some of the American words, they were about "bombs bursting in air." Not bad but just a start.

I thought the region would make more about the battles and the anthem that came out of them. But no. Maybe because America lost. Or, of course, because the best fights were here but the anthem was written in Baltimore. Francis Scott Key, who seems to have been a gentle, curly-haired man with a long nose who wrote poetry when he wasn't going through law books, went out to a British warship to try to release an American prisoner. The British treated him kindly even though he probably read them his poems. They even let him sit in on a meeting to plan the next stage of the battle. Which was his undoing, really, because he now knew all the plans and they couldn't let him off the ship.

He pushed his fingers in his ears and kept out of the way as the British opened fire. He admired the way the shells were set to explode at or over the target. And with nothing else to do, he thought up another poem. Next morning he finished it off on the back of an envelope and called it *Defense of Fort M'Henry*, which as a title isn't very good at all. He was inspired because when the smoke cleared, there still flying over the fort was the American flag, in those days with 15 stars and 15 stripes.

One good and one bad idea followed. The first was to change the name to *The Star-Spangled Banner*. The second was to pick a tune for it that was almost impossible to sing because of its range. Nevertheless, Americans get terribly proud when they hear it, which is at every available opportunity including the start of baseball matches, and they leap up and place their hands on their wallets. But they could have been quicker about it. Key wrote his rotten poem in September 1814. It didn't become the American anthem until March 1931. In fact, until then there had been no national anthem at all. Curious but true.

Léo Woodland

Well, America may have lost the war but it is winning Niagara Falls. The water erodes the rock and little by little the falls move into the USA. The moment to be there will be when they wear right back to Lake Erie and the water comes rushing in. I will buy tickets for that.

It's a sad place, Niagara Falls. Two sad places, really, because there's a town of the same name on both banks. The Canadians have the best of the spectacle and all the tourists. They have had the good grace to leave the river bank unscathed. Just one street back, however, is a UNESCO heritage site of bad taste and neon. Try the Nightmares Fear Factory, for instance. For "more than 30 years" it has been "thrilling, chilling and out right [sic] terrorizing victims of all ages. Your time with us will depend on you; and will range from 15 seconds to 15 minutes."

"It was the best haunted house I have ever been in," a man called Thomas "from Canada" enthuses in the brochure, adding as confirmation "And I go to lots of haunted houses."

It's in competition with The Haunted House, "a terrifying experience" with "a ghost in every corner, a skeleton in every closet, every kind of ghoul imaginable; you'll be too frightened to be nervous!" If that's not for you, try the SpongeBob Squarepants 4-D ride and "get ready for a hilarious and zany adventure as SpongeBob chases a robotic double of Patrick through Bikini Bottom."

Things are calmer, less neon, across the water on the American side. It must be the first time Canada has been glitzier than the USA. American Niagara Falls is a working town, resentful perhaps of the fun going on across the bridge but making the most of it. The best we could find was the Niagara Power Project Power Vista. We weren't sure why "power" needed to be there twice but we were impressed that the advertisement printed FREE FAMILY FUN ALL YEAR ROUND in four colors.

Niagara Falls proposed once that it should be headquarters of the United Nations. Like much else, it came to nothing. I listened to a radio documentary about the place. "The classic story of America is the story of people who started with nothing, pulled themselves up by their bootstraps, and made something of themselves," the narrator said. "The story of the town of Niagara Falls is the opposite. The town started with something huge—the Falls—and built nothing lasting from it. The modern history of Niagara Falls can be divided roughly into three phases: schemers who came in trying to exploit the Falls for tourism, and failed; schemers who came in and tried to exploit the Falls for hydroelectric power, who've all gone; and the people who are left in Niagara Falls today."

The schemers included those who in 1827 advertised they'd send wild animals over the Falls. People expected lions and tigers but got a buffalo, two foxes, a raccoon and 15 geese…"but no matter—everyone made money". Ditto, doubtless, at the Niagara Wedding Chapel; it performs 2,000 weddings a year, mostly second marriages. Each lasts seven minutes. Guests for the following wedding are taking their seats before the first lot have left.

"What could be more dramatic and romantic than having the majestic Niagara Falls as the background to your wedding or honeymoon?" the tourist brochure asks. "It's easy to get married at the Falls. Go to any city clerk or town clerk's office in New York State which issue marriage licenses. The fee is $40. Both parties…must present a driver's license or passport or birth certificate." The city was honeymoon capital of world until competition arrived thanks to cheap air travel. But the legend remains.

Those who can't find happiness throw themselves into the water. They do it mostly on Mondays, least on Wednesdays. The peak time is 4pm. September is the favorite month, October the least. Someone has kept all these figures. Someone has also noted that most suicides stare at the water and take off their shoes before they leap. It's as much a business as everything else: body-rescuers get $100 a corpse.

Half the population has left since the 1950s. More than 60 percent of those who remain are elderly. Same in Buffalo. We crossed from the prosperity of the Niagara Park trail in Canada, with its horizon-filling white houses and their three garages, into the sadness of Buffalo. To commit suicide there, said the composer Harold Arlen, would be redundant.

I picked up the *Buffalo News*. It reported that "a fight between two teenage boys over a stolen bicycle resulted in the stabbing of one of the combatants. Buffalo police officers said when they arrived on the scene, they found the 15-year-old victim with a knife in his back. The victim, police said, had confronted a 13-year-old boy about the bike and punched him in the face. Friends and family joined in the fray, and the 13-year-old pulled a knife out of his right pocket, according to police. When the victim rushed at the 13-year-old, he was stabbed two or three times, the police added."

Léo Woodland

There was another story. A man was held up at gunpoint and, seeing no point in resisting, handed over the $20 he had. The thief was grateful but shot him in the hip anyway to stop his running after him. What made it depressing was that incidents that elsewhere would have taken the front page were so mundane that they made a news-in-brief section deep inside the paper.

We felt sorry for Buffalo. Its wide streets showed the importance of the port. Or the port that was. Now there were closed warehouses and factories, boarded up and decaying. It was heart-tearing after the dripping prosperity of the riverside parkway on the Canadian side. Business after business had closed. The X-ray company...abandoned. Parts manufacturers, specialist toolmakers...gone. Empty lots with weeds pushing through gaps in the concrete stood where men worked and a city's heart beat. The roads were rutted and holed. Depressed people in inexpensive clothing walked sullenly, although they broke into smiles when greeted. There was still something there.

"The best thing to do with Buffalo is go there and get out as fast as you can," said Big John at Daisies Cafe in Lackawanna, on the far side of town. Lackawanna—the name chosen by Seneca Indians who sold their reservation, I don't know how willingly, in 1842—is better off than Buffalo but not much. John was a big, ebullient man who owned the cafe. He wore a chef's checkered pants. "I went down south, to have a look where everything's supposed to better. I came back. You make it in business here and you can make it anywhere. This area's been hit pretty hard this past twenty years. Steelworks closed here in Lackawanna two decades back and the place is still feeling it. They're trying to replace it with technological stuff, you know, minimum-wage assembly work, that sorta stuff, and that's starting to work, but..." He shrugged.

Across the road stood the dome of Lackawanna's basilica. When it was built in 1925 it was the largest dome in the USA outside the US Capitol Building. It's a magnificent place which has its roots in a tiny crossroads church that had an asylum for orphan boys beside it. That was around 1850. Five or six years later a new asylum was built where the church stands now. A new man, Nelson H. Baker, took over the orphanage, expanding it until by 1919 there was also a boys' school, a working boys' home, an infants' home, a maternity home, and a hospital. He named the basilica after the shrine to Our Lady of Victories in Paris, which he had visited. He died in July 1936 and he's now in a holding stage before being named a saint.

Baker reckoned there were a thousand angels in the basilica, but he underestimated. It seems nobody has counted them all but there are between 1,500 and 2,000. There are also 14 Stations of the Cross, significant points of a church for a Roman Catholic, with figures close to life size. The first time I heard about Stations of the Cross was from a retired trade union leader called Ron Todd. This has nothing to do with cycling but the story so amused me that I'll tell you anyway. Ron was a demon figure in the British union movement in the 1970s, a barrow boy lookalike who fought for workers' rights at Ford in east London and rose to fight for them in the national congress of unions. He was far from extreme but he had an edge and a broad London accent that made him easy to caricature.

Well, everybody has an unknown side and Ron's was that he was an expert on Victorian music hall and that he collected autographs. He had them from many of the world's leaders, including John F. Kennedy and Russian presidents. Many he acquired by trading surplus signatures in his own collection.

"The most valuable autograph you could get was Margaret Thatcher's," he told me. "Get that and you could swap it for almost anything. So when I saw in advertisements that there was a signature I wanted, I'd offer to swap it for one of Thatcher's. Which I didn't always have, of course. So I used to write to her as leader of the trade union movement and say 'Dear Mrs. Thatcher, I think the time has come for world revolution.' And she, of course, she had no sense of humor and she'd write me back this long explanation of why I was wrong. And I got the signature I wanted! And I got it several times, too. She never caught on."

At Evangola State Park, on the banks of Lake Erie, a woman towing a dog from her tricycle told us we were in for a hard time. We were going to Titusville, we said. Then you'll be going up a lot of hills, she replied. We shrugged and smiled patronizingly. We are super-fit knights of the road. We laugh at such things. Next morning we went up a lot of hills. Long, hard and repeated hills. And why Titusville? Because there, across in Pennsylvania, the modern world began. The story goes back to the Bible.

Léo Woodland

Which reminds me, before I go further, that we hadn't been going long when we ran through a series of farms which had something indefinably different about them. Something missing. And then, moments before we saw a man in a floppy black hat and blue overalls

The Amish live just as they did 200 years ago—but what were cars doing outside their houses?

plowing with four horses, we realized there were no tractors, no pickups and no electricity lines. We were in Amish country, in a world before petroleum.

I always pronounced it Aymish. Apparently it's Ah-mish. And their origin is as much Swiss as German. I only know that because I looked it up afterwards. And then I found that a man called Jakob Ammann thought his neighbors in Switzerland were drifting too far from the true word and ought to be called to order. You can guess the kind of man he was when I tell you that he insisted wives have nothing to do with their husbands, not even eating with them, if they didn't pray and behave properly.

From Ammann's name came the adjective Amish and the greatest number of them in the USA are in Ohio (official state drink: tomato juice, decided in 1965), and in Pennsylvania. Without being snooty, they consider themselves the chosen race and a royal priesthood and they have as little to do with the world as they can. They try not to use high-voltage electricity because a bishop rejected it in 1920. They spread fertilizer and they're allowed to hire although not own cars but they use horses to pull farm equipment that would run perfectly well on gasoline.

Riding past one farm we came across an Amish carriage, wooden with two wheels, a roof and space for two behind a single horse. In it was a woman called Verna, dressed in shades of blue, like a nun, with a covering for her hair. It was impossible to guess her age.

"We've been here for three generations," she said.

"And where were you previously?" I hoped to hear it was Germany or Switzerland.

"We came from Pennsylvania."

"What led you to leave there?"

"I can't rightly say, sir."

She wasn't comfortable, not in her wagon but talking to us. Behind her, though, was a fence, two horizontal wooden rails painted white, and beyond that a single-story house. Out of a door at the end came a broom-bearded man in blue overalls and a straw hat. Dan, Verna's husband, was as smiling as Verna was severe.

"There are maybe 60 families hereabouts," he said. "We live this way because we want to. It's a simple life, one we value."

We asked if Amish children valued it as much. They wouldn't have seen much television, not having electricity, and they were largely educated within the community—although only to an extent because the Amish believe extensive schooling isn't needed for a life on the land—but they did live in a world of enticement.

"They don't often leave but, when they do, they come back once they've tried the rest of the world. Even the best lawns have brown patches," Dan said.

Another man joined us. Like Dan, his beard stuck out bristle-like at right angles to his face. He wore the same style of blue overalls and white straw hat. Jacob was more smiling than Dan but he spoke less.

Did France have farms, they wanted to know. And how far were we from Hungary, which was where one of their neighbors was born? "I've never been abroad," Dan said hurriedly. Then he asked: "What are gas prices like where you live?"

We told him American prices struck us as spectacularly low.

"Folk hereabouts complain they're too high," he said. An unusual comment, I thought, for a man I assumed went everywhere behind a horse. Or was that car in the driveway not a visitor's after all? Did the Amish really have no power, no electricity, no engine power? It seemed the most tactful way to ask about the car.

"We have a tractor," Dan answered, "but only to drive the belt on a woodcutter."

"And how do you get on in the winter?"

"We get snow six feet deep. We spend a lot of time hauling logs and plowing snow!"

We'd hoped to hear Pennsylvania Dutch, the Amish language. Bill Bryson observed that "The name is an accident of history. From the early 18th century to almost the end of the 19th, *Dutch* in American English was applied not just to the language of Holland and its environs, but to much else that was bewilderingly foreign, most especially the German language—doubtless in confusion with the German word *Deutsch*. To the Pennsylvania Dutch, the language is called Muddersrschprooch. To scholars and the linguistically fastidious, it is Pennsylvania German. For a century and a half Pennsylvania German was largely ignored by scholars. As the linguist and historian C. Richard Beam has put it: 'In an age when there are billions of dollars available for trips to the moon and destruction abroad, it is very difficult to procure even a few hundred dollars to help finance the production of a dictionary of the language of the oldest and largest German language island on the North American continent.'"

Anyway, as I was saying, the story of Titusville goes back to the Bible. There were burning bushes, strange lights in the desert, vegetation that burned but didn't perish. Now we know it was petroleum surfacing in the heart of the Middle East oil field before vaporizing and catching fire. The Indians of what is now Pennsylvania used crude oil for body paint or to treat wounds. Someone worked out how to create kerosene, but that was good only for lamps and it was hard to get your hands on enough to be commercially exciting. The Pennsylvania Rock Oil Company tried digging, but that didn't work. And in the summer of 1856 the man who owned the company, George Bissell, happened to shelter from the New York sun, staring into the window of a druggist's shop on Broadway.

The shop sold patent medicine that contained rock oil. The packets showed wells used to extract salt. Could he do the same for oil? Bissell's banker was James Townsend. Townsend shared a hotel with an out-of-work jack-of-all-trades called Edwin Drake. Drake had a way with a story and a knack for placing himself at the center of events. Townsend was impressed. He was impressed too that Drake had a railroad pass. Drake may not turn out any good as a searcher of oil but at least he would cost nothing in rail fares.

Titusville in December 1857 had just 125 people, most in the lumber business. Drake recruited a blacksmith called "Uncle Billy" Smith who drilled and drilled and spent all the firm's money. The company had just written to fire him when he struck oil. Bissell wrote to his wife: "The whole population are crazy almost…I never saw such excitement. The whole western country are thronging here and fabulous prices are being offered for lands in the vicinity where there is a prospect of getting oil."

There was no excitement for us. Quite the opposite. It rained and it rained harder and it grew cold and we grew cold. Cold to the point of shivering, of knowing something dangerous was happening. We didn't know how many hotels there were in Titusville but the first was good enough. We left puddled footsteps across the foyer and stood long and delighted under the shower. Only half an hour later did we feel normal.

Well, Titusville is pleasant enough. The woman in the tourist office did her best to get us to buy antiques before conceding that, no, a bike was no way to carry a chest of drawers or a table. How about a restaurant in an old railroad car? Or how about, I suggested, the brew pub listed in the town guide? That was more like it. America is far from impressive for its national beers but it does a decent job with local ones. In Cleveland they have one named after the day the river caught fire.

"It was so polluted that sparks from a train on the bridge set fire to it," Aaron Maughan said with a not-too-embarrassed smirk. He worked in a bike shop there.

The river fire is so notorious that 30 years later—it happened on June 22, 1969—people still ask about it. The man restoring the area along the Cuyahoga river said: "You'd think that people would forget about it after all this time. But no. I had a visitor here from Russia recently and the first thing he wanted to see was where the river burned." The city's fathers probably aren't wild about Burning River pale ale, although

I thought it was pretty good. But then they're probably not thinking about the taste.

The beer in Titusville at the Blue Canary also went down well. That's the brew pub and restaurant in the center of town. But more interesting was Drake Well museum a stiff walk away. It was there that "Captain" Drake first extracted oil in commercial quantities, production that the Civil War did little to disrupt. Nor did it disrupt the greed of those who raced there.

Daniel Yergin, in *The Prize*, wrote: "Nothing revealed the feverish pitch of speculation better than the strange story of the town of Pithole, on Pithole Creek, some 15 miles from Titusville. A first well was struck in the dense forest land there in January 1865; by June, there were four flowing wells and people fought their way in on roads already clogged with the barrel-laden wagons. 'The whole place,' said one visitor, 'smells like a corps of soldiers when they have the diarrhea.'

"The land speculation seemed to know no bounds. One farm that had been virtually worthless a few months earlier was sold for $1.3 million in July 1865, and then resold for two million dollars in September. What had once been an unidentifiable spot in the wilderness had become a town of fifteen thousand people, two banks, two telegraph offices, a newspaper, a waterworks, a fire company, scores of boarding houses and businesses, more than fifty hotels.

"But then, a couple of months later, the oil production abruptly gave out. By January 1866, only a year from the first discovery, thousands had fled. The town that had sprung up overnight from the wilderness was totally deserted. Fires ravaged the buildings and the wooden skeletons that were left were torn down to be used for building elsewhere or burned as kindling by farmers. A parcel of land in Pithole that sold for $2 million in 1865 was auctioned for $4.37 in 1878."

Many lost their money. Bissell, though, became wildly rich and among other things provided a gym for Dartmouth college, insisting it had six bowling alleys—"in remembrance of disciplinary troubles into which he had fallen as an undergraduate because of his indulgence in this sinful sport." Drake lost everything and fell ill. He wrote to a friend: "If you have any of the milk of human kindness left in your bosom for me or my family, send me some money." Pennsylvania finally gave him a small pension for what he achieved for the state and the world.

The park at Titusville has reconstructed the pump and oil pipe. People back then didn't realize they were living in the past, of course. They didn't bother to save what they no longer needed.

The road to Titusville was indeed pretty hilly.

Don't get the idea of a well the size of Texas or the Middle East. Drake was happy with a steam-and-chain machine that turned a metal flywheel the height of a man. Its six spokes were curved elegantly. As it turned, a pump sucked oil out of the ground. It poured, green rather than black, out of a pipe the size you'd use on a garage forecourt and it delivered at about the same speed. It didn't spurt or pulse or do anything exciting. It poured at the rate you'd fill a bucket.

"We don't have the rights to extract oil," the guide told us. He was a retired teacher of reading and writing, a man whose interest in history meant the job at Titusville was a dream come true. "In a state park it wouldn't be allowed anyway, so we recycle the oil and there where you see it coming out of the pipe is the precise point where petroleum was first pumped from the earth anywhere in the world."

There is something impressive about standing at the point where the world changed, especially when that point is no larger than an oil barrel.

Steph paid for that hard, wet ride into Titusville. We gambled that the busier road from Titusville to Erie would be flatter and have a shoulder. But... The shoulder was narrow, cracked and crumbling and a never-ending hill thrust itself at us minutes after starting. The sun shone but Steph's face was as pallid as fog as only tenacity got her to the top, drawn, shattered and in tears.

"Just let me recover," she asked, arms resting on the handlebars, head dropped. I waited with her for perhaps 10 minutes. We grew cold and I suggested the porch of a nearby house.

"I just don't want to have to talk to anyone," she said, asking not to add her to her upset.

To me, the cause was simple: tiredness, certainly, but also lack of food. I took a pile of her luggage and we rode on to Gina's café near Union City, there to down eggs on toast and an ocean of coffee. Across the room, a woman of 42 (she told us her age) was saying: "First time I got married for love. Second time I got married for stoopid. Third time's gonna be for lots and lots o' money."

A man in a checkered shirt sat opposite. He looked like a boy who thought Santa was bringing toffees but got socks instead. "Yep," he said. "Gotta be right there." There was a silence before he added: "What about that son o' yours?"

"Wanted to join the Marines," the woman said. "Wanted it the roughest, toughest there was. I said 'You see that Traveling Wall that came by?' You know that wall they bring round with the names of all the dead military on it?"

The man nodded that he did.

"I pointed to them all. Marine, marine, army, marine, army.... Ain't that just what a mother wants? I said 'Why don't you join the navy or the air force?'"

"Sure enough," the man said. "Navy or the air force. They was all here a while back and the army they were in pup tents in a field some place. The navy, they was all in hotels downtown. That's the way you gotta do it."

"Well, he's joining the air force now."

The man stirred more sugar into his coffee, took a sip, didn't like it, stirred in some more.

"You tell him not to be a pilot," he said. "You become a pilot and folks gonna shoot at you. You tell him to join the air force and play stupid. That's the way to do it."

At Erie we camped on the fine sand of the beach. There is nothing more satisfying by water than to read of shipping disasters. I settled into the armchair of a café beside the hideous RV park across the road and read of the *Wesee*, "a long dark ship with a high bow and, at the stem, a single smokestack." She had previously been called the *Orion*, getting the new name after being rebuilt in 1917. Out on the lake, the *Wesee* caught fire at midnight and, the crew unable to put out the blaze, ran aground on Middle Sister Island. The 18 men and a female cook escaped on two yawl boats. They had barely reached the shore when two starving fishermen from Port Clinton, Ohio, ran up to see them. They'd hoped the *Wesee* was coming to rescue them and were doubtless disappointed when it turned out to be yet another wreck, and a wreck with a further 19 hungry mouths to feed.

The fishermen had been transporting a cabin cruiser from Sandwich, Ontario, to Port Clinton when it sprang a leak. They had reached the island, where they lit a fire and scavenged for what they could eat: birds, onions, a single apple and a radish. They'd been there four and a half days.

The 19 from the *Wesee* heard this with sinking hearts. The single apple and the lone radish had gone and there was no certainty they'd find more birds or onions. They had contemplated the issue for some time when over the horizon came the steamer *Conneaut*. Its lookouts had spotted the flames of the *Wesee* and come to look. The shipwrecked sailors were saved. And, should you have been worrying, the cabin cruiser was recovered and delivered to her owner. The *Wesee*, meanwhile, lies in scattered lumps on rocks northwest of Middle Sister.

You'd think that was excitement enough for Erie, but no. I was delighted to find that not only did three railways come to town but that each had a track of different width. It played havoc with connections and passengers' lives but the town liked it because it made a packet out of selling meals and hotel rooms. A passenger from Buffalo to Cleveland had to change at the Pennsylvania border, then again in Erie. Many missed trains. Many more were delayed. But the greater the delay, the larger the profit.

And then somebody proposed making the lines the same size. Trains could run straight through and nobody would need to spend the night any more. This wasn't what Erie wanted to hear and the mayor, a man called Alf King, led mobs in setting fire to bridges, ripping up track and generally being unpleasant. King and 150 protesters he had appointed as "special police constables" went to the bridge crossing State and French streets and cut sections out. People seven miles away in Harborcreek tore up tracks. Three days later the new line was finished to the city limits and Harbor Creek tore it out again, knocked down a bridge and demolished a level crossing.

On December 27, 1853, a crowd ripping up tracks outside Harborcreek stopped a train of rail officials. One of them pulled out a gun and fired. A man fell to the ground and the crowd rushed the train. The official was dragged aboard, the engineer put the train in reverse and it "headed at full speed for the state line."

To be honest, we'd have enjoyed the Great Lakes more if we'd seen them. They were mostly hidden behind rich people's houses. The sort of houses you thought existed only in Jackie Collins paperbacks. And we'd have enjoyed ourselves better had every middle-age crisis not been out on his Harley-Davidson. Harley-Davidsons cost a great deal. Overhearing a café conversation, that seems why only the middle-aged buy them. Only they can afford them. And having got one, they take out the mufflers that I assume the factory fits and make an earsplitting noise that forces you to look round and see what they've bought. They sound like a million amplified Dutchmen clearing their throats.

What you also see is a looks limit for Harley riders. How ugly they are before they shave their heads and grow beards and put on a pirate's bandanna, I don't know. Maybe during the week when they're respectable accountants and dentists they look pretty normal. Except, of course, for the great, obligatory paunch. At weekends, they dash into telephone boxes and rip off their day clothes and emerge not in blue tights and a cape but in leathers and pointed boots and the sort of mean look you associate with Mexican bandits in the 19th century.

Harley riders, always male, make a point of looking mean and ugly. They sit back on their machines, leaning against a backrest as though they're in a barber's chair. Their legs spread wide. They greet the world first with their feet and then with their crotch. It may be their prettiest aspect. Their wives and girlfriends on the pillion rarely look any better. It is good to see ugly people making each other happy.

To get back to the lakes, though.... At Lorain, there's an excellent view from a small park on a cliff. The weather was good and sunbathers were making the most of it, including a couple of advanced years who'd taken their folding chairs into the water and were sitting there peering back at the beach as though they'd been cut off by the tide. What amused me more was that the beach lay in the shadow, or would have had the sun been in that direction, of a power station. An ugly one it was, too, with a high, round and slightly conical chimney rising almost from the beach itself, a shabby building of corrugated metal behind it and then the great box of the main installation, all mysteriously bulging as though its intestines had poked out.

We ate sandwiches watching the sunbathers and admiring the power station. A man in blue overalls, thin with silver hair and jangling keys in his right hand, walked by, smiled, walked on. He came up again as I stretched my legs.

"They sure do it to tease us older guys, don't they?" he asked, out of Steph's hearing. I wasn't sure I wanted to be an "older guy" but in America you become a "senior" at 50. People were repeatedly less surprised that we were riding across America than that we were doing it as "seniors". Or that I was, anyway.

"Who does what to tease us?", I asked, giving in to the description.

He nodded down at the beach.

"Pushing their bikini bottoms down to show the crack of their ass," he said. I expected to see a girl with a triangle of fabric round her knees. I saw nothing that surprised, shocked or teased. I was more amused by what he'd said.

"Where you coming from?" he asked.

I said I was French.

"Oh gee, they sunbathe *nood* over there, don't they?"

He wasn't dribbling but I was sure his keys were jangling more.

We traveled on busy roads from Pennsylvania into Ohio, passing still more funeral parlors on the way. America is well provided with funeral parlors, all of them temples of the dead with slightly sickly names. The National Funeral Directors' Association lists 20,300 of them and that's just their members. There are several thousand more.

Ohio is different. It's quieter and it's flatter for a start. We rode south on narrow roads that ran vertically or horizontally. That is, you rode down the map or you rode across it. The notion of riding diagonally seems not to have occurred and the rare through routes that went that way did so not in a straight line but a succession of right-angled bends. The roads were narrower but the drivers were as patient and as cautious as ever. American cyclists think their drivers there are awful. We had never met such kindness, courtesy and care. We always thought German drivers the best but Americans were better. When a sign said Stop, they stopped. Everyone stopped, often on all four sides of a junction. I always hoped they'd settle priorities with gunfire but they just smiled and waved each other on and eventually someone blushingly agreed to go first.

"Watch out for pickup drivers," someone warned us. There is a connotation in being a pickup driver in America, one we never defined but which wasn't flattering. We weren't sure, therefore, when a black pickup, all five liters of it and gleaming with chrome and steel, drove the other way with the driver shouting at us through his window. On a bike, you hear people are yelling but rarely make out what they say. But shouting in general isn't good news. We looked at each other, shrugged and rode on. Moments later we heard tires squealing as the truck made a tight turn. The engine picked up a tone as it accelerated after us. This looked like trouble.

The black monster pulled up beside us and slowed. The driver wound down the opposite window, leaned over and, watching us and watching for oncoming traffic, bellowed: "If you guys are looking for somewhere to spend the night, you're welcome at our place."

There is an exceptional willingness to help in America. Stop with a map and it takes of all three seconds for someone to offer. Ride into a village and someone will call "Looking for some place to eat, huh?" and give directions. Cyclists either look perpetually haggard and hungry or it's an excuse to offer assistance. The man in the pickup wasn't the first, either. A sailor painting his yacht for summer strolled over as I waited for Steph in Port Ontario. Like everyone, he wanted to know where we were going, where we'd been, how far we rode a day. I answered all that and gave him a slip of paper with our blog address. In return he gave me a card of his own and said: "Don't suppose you're going to make it as far as Oregon but we'd be pleased to put you up."

A day or two later, as we rode into the wind, a flatback truck slowed and the driver offered a lift. And seemed surprised that we chose to bow our backs than sit up in the cab and take it easy. People in Europe say this friendliness, this cheerfulness, is superficial. I don't think it is. But even if it were, wouldn't you rather be among people who are superficially friendly and cheerful than authentically miserable?

Anyway, as I was saying, Ohio is flat. This bit, anyway. The roads were well surfaced and they ran at right angles to each other. They passed small, neat farms with red Dutch barns—there were 10,000 Dutch immigrants in Ohio in 1900—all the farms of a human size. There are 76,000 farms in the state, we found, and three in every five are smaller than 50 acres. That's why those white houses with their neighboring silos.

"This is a working countryside," Steph said. "Pickup trucks carry things here. They're working. They're not trophies like they are down by the coast." The area may never be prosperous and perhaps it never was. But it looked constant. The economy was more balanced and looked to have survived the recession better. In New York we saw abandoned businesses and closed homes, all waiting forlornly for a buyer. Buffalo had steel and chemicals and a port but when all that failed it was left with nothing. Here in rural Ohio there were few towns and no signs of luxury. But equally there was no devastation either. Villages were small but vibrant, many with a little white church outside which the word of God was spelled in bowing plastic letters clipped to a rack.

"This is the first time we've seen an active economy," Steph observed.

Not that Hans is contributing to it much. His days of active contribution are over and now he rides a bike, like us, anywhere that amuses him. Hans lives in Celina and that's why we were riding south through Ohio rather than west, the route that would get us to the Pacific. Our friendship goes back four years, to my first and unsuccessful attempt to straddle North America like a lean-thighed Colossus. I passed through Pippa Passes, in Kentucky. The place is remarkable for three things: its grubby youth hostel, now closed, for being where Robert Browning wrote:

> *The lark's on the wing;*
> *The snail's on the thorn;*
> *God's in his Heaven—*
> *All's right with the world!*

and for being where I met Hans. And Hans is remarkable for having saved America and the world from the Red Menace.

(I should add here that Robert Browning was a splendid poet but that he lacked a certain contact with the more rumbustious world. Read the second verse of *Pippa Passes* and you'll see what I mean. Somewhere along the line he gets the idea that a "twat" is part of a nun's clothing rather than, let's say, her body. He went years before anybody had the nerve to point it out.)

Hans is a hefty, square-shaped smiling man who's lived in Ohio since 1958 but still has some of his German accent. With dry humor he told me he learned bricklaying in Germany "because it seemed a promising trade after the war." Having rebuilt Germany, he moved to America, where his brother lived.

"They still had the draft then and from the moment you came into the country, you were eligible for it. But only the army had the draft and I decided to apply for the navy. So I applied and they said to come back once I spoke some English, because I didn't speak a word. So then I went to the air force, and in a big naval base like Newport News where I was, they weren't getting any recruits so the guy just stood over me and said 'Put an X here' and 'Put an X there', and I was in.

"They sent me to the supplies department and I went to a supplies school and once I'd qualified they welcomed us all and told us not to expect any promotion.

"'Why?'

"'Because we always have more people than we need.'

"'Then why did you recruit us?'

"'Because in supplies, nobody ever re-enlists.'

"So one day the air force got a computer and this thing filled a huge room, with flashing lights and whirling tapes. They wanted us stores people to run a stores computer and I stayed 20 years."

He was once even posted to Germany. "We were there to hold back the red menace," he said with an air of mockery, not convinced there'd ever been one, not sure his antics in Germany would have left him fit to fight it if there had been. The 200 euros a year pension he gets from his bricklaying days may pay for his drinking now but it wouldn't have then. "We used to have a few beers—well, maybe more than a few—and then we'd look at each other and say 'You realize we're the last defense against the communist hordes, don't you?'"

He still rides with a trailer marked "Hans Rehrmann, Msgt. USAF (Ret)."

To reach him meant crossing Lima. Few places have had quite so exciting a history. For a start, oil was found there in 1885 and set off the Oil Boom of Northwest Ohio. It came just a year after discovery of natural gas in Findlay, 40 miles north. Oil fever spread and boom towns sprang up as they had around Titusville. Lima was a world-class producer between 1887 and 1905, filling 300 million barrels. Oil from Lima lit the Chicago Worlds Fair. Then, just as in Pennsylvania, it ran out and by 1910 there was barely any left.

That wasn't the last bad news for Lima. John Dillinger, who blamed the world for his venereal disease and the painful treatment it needed, had robbed the Citizens National Bank in Bluffton of $2,100. It was 1933 and he was locked up in stone block built beside the sheriff's home in North Street in Lima, near the square. Dillinger didn't take locking up lightly and he arranged for three friends to drop by. The sheriff, Jess Sarber, had just finished pork chops and mashed potatoes. He was reading a story in the *Lima News* about George "Machine Gun" Kelly when in came men claiming they were officers from Michigan to see Dillinger. Sarber was prepared to help but he wanted their badges. The men pulled out guns instead and shot Sarber as he reached for the Colt .38 in his top drawer. He dropped to the floor and died.

Just as unpleasant were the notoriously violent Black Legion, part of the Ku Klux Klan. It had so many supporters around Lima that a parade in August 1923 drew 100,000. Civil rights didn't come easily to Lima, especially efforts to desegregate the swimming pool. You can tell the kind of town it was when I tell you the local paper campaigned against a public library in the 1950s because anyone who wanted a book should buy one.

No such excitement for us. The only thing I remember is a café where a slim and elegant waitress had a Caribbean beach scene tattooed on one calf.

"Is it real or stuck on?"

She said it was real.

"I'm thinking of having it extended up my leg."

"What, sky, clouds and seagulls?"

"Yes, right up to here," she said, hoisting her skirt all of half an inch to mid-thigh level. And then she said: "By the way, if you want to use the bathroom, you can't because the pipe's blocked."

We called at the library in Celina. Libraries are the pride of the country, spacious, clean and well kept. They are a joy to be in. They are signposted from the center of town. The librarians are smiling and helpful. Offer them a couple of dollars for library funds, for after all we are not taxpayers here, and they blush and say: "But you really don't have to." We know we don't. That's what makes it even more worthwhile.

The librarian at Celina asked what brought us to town. I said I'd met a cyclist in Kentucky four years back. I got no further before she said: "You mean Hans? Hans Rehrmann?"

I said I did.

She didn't quite say "Why didn't you say so, then?" She said: "Hans is pretty well known round here." Hans's version is that he's pretty well known because the local paper has nothing else to write about.

"It's pretty peaceful round here," he said as he drank another beer under the disapproving eye of his wife, Joan. We said we were having an alcohol rub before a game of hillbilly golf, a game best played half-cut which demands weighted strings are thrown so that they wrap round a horizontal bar several places away.

"When we turn on the TV news from Dayton, it's all this person being murdered or that person being beaten up or robbed. On our own local TV from Lima, it's just council news, what's happened at city hall. It's not just peaceful: it's pretty boring. But that's what makes it a nice place to live."

Didn't used to be, though. Hans remembers a sign at the entrance to town that read: "Nigger, don't let the sun go down on you here."

Steph, Hans and I rode to Monroeville, across the border in Indiana. To the world, Monroeville is neither here nor there. To cyclists it's up there with Paris, New York and London. Why? Because Monroeville goes so far out of its way to welcome cyclists that it has opened its park and its sports pavilion to them. A yellow sign on its door gives numbers to call. We called and a bustling little man of retirement age arrived and fussed about like the White Rabbit, hurrying, hurrying, hurrying with nothing to do.

Outside, the park waited for our tents. Beside it, a white rotunda surrounded by flowers and set off by a stately clock on a metal pillar. Inside, a Stars and Stripes hung vertically on the wall with a sign confirming that "cross country bikers stay free of charge." On another wall was the certificate presented to the town by the Adventure Cycling Association. "In 1976," it says, Monroeville Community Park Board "opened up the community center to touring bicyclists for free. They keep a log book for cyclists, and hundreds of touring cyclists have found reprieve from the road in their kindness."

The Adventure Cycling Association started when a handful of friends thought it would be fun to celebrate America's bicentennial in 1976 by cycling from the Pacific to the Atlantic Coast at Williamsburg, where those settlers arrived. They would follow history backwards, from west to east, probably because they lived in Missoula, in Montana, which is more west than east. They called their idea the Bikecentennial and wondered if anybody else would take part. Four thousand of them did, following detailed maps of backroads routes across the continent. Having created so much, the founders were reluctant to let it go. They formed a formal association and set about planning other cross-country routes away from the traffic and interstates that would otherwise plague a cyclist's life. We were following one of those routes, south of the Lakes and then north to the Canadian border before turning left for the Pacific.

It didn't take long for towns to notice cyclists where previously there had been none. Some watched with disinterest, others thoughtfully. The best realized cyclists bought food and drink. They stayed in hotels and bed-and-breakfasts. They didn't hurry through like car-borne tourists.

Towns which had no hotel or bed-and-breakfast opened the park to campers. It cost nothing to maintain grass that was already there. Some went further and Monroeville has become an example to others. There are no records of how many passed through in the first years but around 1,300 have stayed since 1990. We are the second group this year, just behind two Belgians.

There are just more than 1,200 people in Monroeville and they're served by the *Monroeville News*. Its editor came running across as we ate breakfast in a café opposite her office. Lois Ternet was a round-faced woman with brown hair and twinkling brown eyes. She bubbles enthusiasm. She has worked at the paper "for decades", she said, its sole employee. It sold as many copies as there are people in the village. "We just cover weddings and things like that." She handed us small wooden fridge stickers in the shape of Indiana. She took our pictures, took notes, and led us into her two-room office. It was cluttered, as a newspaper office should be. On the left wall beside the door was a wide pinboard with a picture of Lance Armstrong, a cartoon, a spray of small colored pennants from the Monroeville Harvest Festival Parade from 1993 to 2007, somebody's red, blue and yellow cycling jersey and two dozen pictures of tired touring cyclists.

"I'll put you up there to join them," she said. We made the front page as well as the clipboard. "It wasn't hard to spot some of this season's earliest cyclists," Lois wrote, "dressed in their bright colored Spandex and all. But this tanned trio, two gents and a blond-haired lady, spoke in accents as well. They stood out amongst the coffee cup clutching town folks at the White Dove Café. They all were apparently enjoying sharing a few laughs and stories, tales of past trips, weather and woes of injuries.

"They seemed like unlikely travel partners—looking for Sticky Buns, the Dan Quayle Museum and the meanings behind quaint names of town and roadside stores along the way. Throw in the love of beer, a game of hillbilly golf and the question why so many Americans fly the flag and you have a quandary. They joke about the image that so many people have and expect of America—like the advertisements on Telly are real!"

The article went on at flattering length, a sign of how little happens in Monroeville. It spilled from the front page on to page four. The lead story on the first of 12 pages started: "As an historic country town,

Monroeville offers just about any kind of business or organization its residents need. Along with clean, quiet neighborhoods, it is a pleasant place to live…" Not much there to upset the locals.

Six pages, half the paper, were given to photos of graduating students. Another told how a young boy won an essay competition. It's easy to see how three cyclists "dressed in their bright colored Spandex and all" might cause such a fuss.

The guest book at the park and another at the White Dove—which the woman in charge wanted to sell because it's exhausting her—made the point over and over: this is small-town America as it used to be, or as you think it used to be. Nita, across town in the Pour Place bar—she had her daughter's date of birth tattooed on one wrist and her son's on the other—had never been anywhere larger than Albuquerque—"and I had to leave because there were too many people and too many streets." This is small-town America. We were just leaving when a slim, elderly woman with blond hair and impeccable diction said: "Strangers in town! Well, welcome!"

I thought of that when I remembered the story that Don told me the previous night. Don was one of two riders, traveling together, with whom we shared the park. The two weren't getting on, sometimes sharing no more than civilities. Don had a long face and wore pants and desert boots; his pal was round-faced with blue eyes and looked a little beaten by life.

"We met when we rode on a group ride," Don said, "but when you're two of 14 you don't know each other like when there's just the two of you." And what they found out, they didn't like.

They walked into town for a beer.

"Lovely place to live," one of them said.

"It's the friendliest place we've been."

"Unless you're black."

"Unless you're black."

They made "phew!" noises. I asked what they meant. They said they'd seen a black man on the street. He appeared to be asking directions. He was certainly an outsider and he was treated as though to keep it that way.

"I heard someone say 'What's that black guy doing here?' And then someone said: 'It's OK, someone else has got him,' as someone went to talk to him."

"And you're sure it wasn't innocent? The white guy wasn't just trying to help?"

The two shrugged. They couldn't be sure. But "sure didn't seem helpful to me," one of them said.

Next morning Don joined us for breakfast opposite the newspaper office and his pal called his daughter for a lift home, officially to sort out domestic problems.

Lois Ternet referred to flags and to Dan Quayle and I ought to explain. In Ohio there were 3.42 flags per kilometer, an extraordinary total helped by their being 500 in the Boulevard of Flags in Eastlake. We saw 940 flags that day, a total unlikely to be beaten and helped by mile after mile of flags hung from every lamppost. I hope it's not beaten, anyway, because counting that high gets pretty wearying.

Nowhere has come anywhere near Ohio. The next best was New York with 1.62 each kilometer. The symbolism of the Stars and Stripes is enormous. Americans seem not to notice, blinded to their own cultural quirks, but the flag is everywhere. There's no pattern to it. It's not as though people in big houses fly them more than those in small. You can go several kilometers without seeing one and then have half a dozen small ones at the entrance to a single house. These are proper flags, too. If I'd counted all the painted ones, the plastic ones, the Stars and Stripes hats and cushion covers, the number would be in the thousands. I asked Sharon Tannahill at the Flag Manufacturers Association of America if she knew how many flags there were in the country. She said she didn't but she knew 150 million flags had been sold and how and when they ought to be flown.

It would interest a psychiatrist to know why so many Americans are keen to boast the obvious, that they're American, and what can safely be taken for granted, that they're proud of America. Do they, like the woman in *Hamlet*, protest too much?

The other reference was to Dan Quayle. In Europe we don't know much about him. He was vice-president, we seem to recall, but whose and when... Well that's asking too much. Although come to think of it, wasn't he the one who said "Not to succeed is to run the risk of failure", and who couldn't spell tomato? Or was it potato?

Actually it was potato, although I don't remember the incident being mentioned at the Dan Quayle Vice-Presidential Museum in

Huntington. So, to remind you, Quayle and a teacher were watching a young boy chalk "potato" on a class blackboard. The boy wrote it correctly but Quayle persuaded him to add a final E, turning to his audience for congratulation. He was given it. Only later did a reporter ask him to say again how he thought the word was written. Quayle was so distressed at a gaffe which he said summarized how the nation thought of him that he gave it a whole chapter in his autobiography.

The opposition made the most of it and Quayle and his president, George Bush, were voted out a few months later. Now, if I weren't honest I'd say that we went to the museum in Huntington regardless, that his reputation didn't sway us. But since the "potatoe" incident—I'm surprised it wasn't called Potatoegate—was all we knew about the man, it would be hard to think up a more wholesome reason.

Indiana, as well as having two towns called Pumpkin Center, has a habit of producing vice-presidents. Five of them over the years. It also, around here, was just a little more rolling. We were finally out of the endless maze of maize and other crops which lay like an unrolled carpet across Ohio and the neighboring areas of Indiana. Villages were more frequent. And there was a town: Huntington. At the entrance, a sign read:

> HUNTINGTON: HOME OF THE 44TH
> VICE PRESIDENT DAN QUAYLE.

Dan Quayle no longer lives there. When he did, he and George Bush announced their election intentions at the town's court building. Quayle emphasized his role as hometown boy by going to one of the town's restaurants. We know that because it said so when we went for lunch there. Now he lives in Phoenix, Arizona, an odd choice of town for a man who had trouble spelling. And an odd choice politically for a man who never rose from the ashes of defeat.

The museum stood in a hefty, religious-looking building with two fluted pillars and a flight of stone steps to a row of wooden doors. Engraved above the entrance is "Dan Quayle Center and Museum." The woman selling tickets had had a quiet morning and looked delighted we'd come.

"It started as a display in the library," said the youthful and enthusiastic curator, who also looked as though life had been quiet and had come down to join us. He was quietly spoken and told us he had spent a year studying in London at the time Chernobyl exploded.

"They were surprised at the response they got and then they wondered about something larger. Well, this used to be a Christian Scientist church and the congregation was down to nine, so they donated it for a museum. Mr Quayle said: 'Don't go filling it with my baby pictures because no one's interested in that', and he suggested a museum dedicated to all vice-presidents."

The vice-president is not an unimportant person. Like the heir to a throne, he is important merely because of who he is. But not because of what he does. The job, said the curator, had only two requirements constitutionally: to breathe and to chair the Senate and cast the deciding vote if there's a tie.

I asked if it had always been that way, since the first president.

"George Washington, you mean?"

"Weren't there a few before him?" I wondered, scraping into the lean barrel of my knowledge of American history. "I thought he was the first after the constitution or something like that."

He smiled and said: "Well, yes, there were early presidents but we never get to learn their names at school."

Which was odd because later that day I picked up the region's tourist brochure. And there, printed white on green, it said:

Samuel Huntington:
Was he the first real president of the United States?

Our country was formed by a constitution that was drafted in 1787, but the first alliance of the thirteen colonies occurred six years before that in 1781 when the Articles of Confederation and Perpetual Union was signed. Many historians now believe that it was this event that created our country and therefore the American presidency.

The document officially named this new collective as 'The United States of America.' Samuel Huntington, the congressman for whom the city and county of Huntington, Indiana, are named, became the de facto president of the United States in Congress Assembled when the articles were ratified. He presided over the Continental Congress until the election of President Thomas McKean. Eight more 'presidents' followed.

When the articles failed, the writers of the U.S. Constitution expressed a desire to form a more perfect union. The perpetual union was specifically cited by Abraham Lincoln 80 years later to justify his forcibly keeping the South from seceding. George Washington became president in 1789. President Samuel Huntington, like the others named before Washington, became a forgotten founder. History isn't about the facts—it's about the interpretation.

We went in expecting to be amused by a museum of the best of the rest. Would it be politics' equivalent of short basketball players? Would it be full of famous people you don't remember ever hearing about? But, no, it was fascinating. We had no idea, for instance, that the original vice-presidents were simply the candidates who lost the presidential election. The winner became president and the runner-up stayed runner-up. Since they came from opposing parties, there was no reason they should get on, and they didn't. The president did his best to stay alive to stop the job going to someone from the opposition. And he did his best, quite easily because there was no requirement to do otherwise, to forget that there was a vice-president at all. It was only in 1974 that the country provided the vice-president with a house in Washington, its having been so improbable that he would ever need to go there.

The museum had explanations and histories of every vice-president since the first. There are campaign posters, photographs, newspapers and an LP called "Spiro Agnew Speaks."

"When I came here," the curator said, "I resolved to turn it into an education center. We got perhaps 500 casual visitors but all between Memorial Day and Labor Day. That left the rest of the year. So we went out to the schools and now we have 10,000 children a year pass through. And I've extended that to going on tours of schools in several states."

By chance, *USA Today* ran an opinion piece across the top of page 11 around the same time. The story, that 18 years ago Quayle spoke for what he'd have called family values and against a fictitious television character who'd had a baby out of wedlock, was less significant than the headline: "Was Dan Quayle—gasp!—right?" It was a given that being right, in his case, was remarkable.

I can't believe Dan Quayle was the buffoon he was painted. He knew his image even before he was elected and, when he was picked, he looked so delighted and fresh-faced that he looked as though he'd won a television game show. The journalists he called to a question-and-answer session came away impressed at his knowledge and sharp wit. For all that cynics say otherwise, you don't get to be vice-president if you're an idiot. We went knowing nothing about Quayle but his potatoes. We saw nothing that trumpeted his intellect or his career. But we left thinking "Surely he can't have been all that bad, can he?"

Well, from the sublime to the ridiculous, or from the ridiculous to the ridiculous, according to your politics, that brought us to the world's largest outdoor privy collection. Maybe the world's *only* outdoor privy collection. America is indeed rich in cultural attractions. The museum isn't signposted. The curator at Dan Quayle's place wasn't sure it was still there. They'd moved it into the museum in town, he thought. But, no, half an hour outside Huntington, unknown except to those who

One man's collection....

know, is a grassy road lined on both sides by privies. Bogs, khazis, lavvies, dunnies. Little outdoor houses of pleasure.

How did they get there, these palaces of poo, all pastel shades, some rickety, some pristine, all locked? Well, it turns out that in 1960 a couple called Lorry and Hy Goldenberg were having work done on their house. The workmen didn't come with the green or blue plastic lavatory you see these days on building sites everywhere. They came with nothing but the male habit of nipping between the trees. Goldenberg set out to buy them something better and to save his wife's blushes, not to mention her trees. A dam was about to flood land close by and folk were selling up. The man in charge of disposing of privies accepted $2 and Goldenberg went to collect his shack. When he got there, there were two because the man said "The first one I found was dreadful." Goldenberg took both for the same price. The authors of *Weird Indiana* say: "Apparently, he believed that two of anything was a collection, and thus started searching far and wide for unique outhouses. Little by little, the long driveway up to his house started to be lined with these structures."

Indiana, by Phyllis Thomas, says: "Building outhouses was a source of employment for many men during the Great Depression. Although comfort and safety were certainly important considerations, aesthetics also played a role. Many were covered with roses and trellises to please the lady of the house. Lest you doubt the current value of outhouses to our society, you should know they are still being built, albeit in more modern forms... The most expensive outhouse in Indiana to date is a four-seat composting toilet in Charlestown State Park in Clark County that set the state back $87,000 when it was built in the mid-1990s. That one, however, is a piker compared to the four-seat outhouse in Glacier National Park in Montana, completed in 1998 at a cost of $1 million."

Along the Goldenberg driveway are ordinary ones, lavvies with heart-shaped peepholes cut into the walls, and one with a bell outside to provoke greater productivity inside. One is a triple-seater, with a child's seat in the middle, for family togetherness. Most cost a dollar or two. The one with a weather vane came to $17 because everyone, of course, wants a privy with a weather vane and someone was bidding against him.

Mrs. Goldenberg may have been less enthusiastic. It is a brave woman who tolerates 17 wooden privies outside her house and the time came after her husband's death in 2000 that she gave many of them to Huntington County Historical Museum. The rest stand on land she donated to create the Tel-Hy Nature Preserve, for which signs stand at the entrance from the road, "Hy", presumably, from her husband's name. The lavvies don't rank, it's true, with the Grand Canyon or the Statue of Liberty. But as a celebration of other men's celebrations, they can't be bettered.

And as a celebration of small-town America, little could better the firemen of Buffalo. Not the big Buffalo back on the shores of the Lakes but the altogether smaller Buffalo at a bend where state road 39 meets state road 16 in Illinois. Not that it seemed like America at first. For a long time we rode on silent roads between high grass that ran to the edge of the road. In America the verge is usually mowed in a strip a meter wide.

Anyway, we were reveling in these restful green lanes, feeling we had dropped into the cover picture of a tourist brochure, when we rode into Buffalo for cold drinks and Sticky Buns. It had been uncommonly warm and America was living outdoors. Girls in bikinis and men with white bellies were going off to swim in the river. People stood about and chatted. It was Memorial Day weekend, but whereas the European equivalent—Armistice—falls in November and therefore starts winter, Memorial Day marks the start of summer. The thermometer was in the mid-30s, although barely anybody here understands Celsius.

Sticky buns are to be had in Buffalo at the back of a gas station. It had tables and a coffee pot and it had passing customers. One of them was a tall, lean man with a contradictory bulging belly who wore dark glasses indoors. He asked the usual questions. Steph answered them while I sulked because he didn't show us the courtesy of removing his glasses.

"Coffee and sugar, they give you energy, right?"

"How many miles you doing?"

"Gotta be in good shape for that, huh?"

Banality, banality. Why he made me so grumpy, I don't know. Steph had had a bad patch with America a while back—"The culture doesn't change," she complained. "We ride and ride but it stays the same. The people are friendly and the scenery is pleasant, but everywhere is just the same"—and maybe I was about to catch it as well. The flat, maize-filled sameness of Ohio had done for Steph. "I know the Plains are going to be like that but I just wasn't prepared for Ohio," she said. Something more general was clearly biting at me.

And then the man changed our day.

"Pancake breakfast across the way, you know that?"

We said we didn't but that it sounded a good thing. We abandoned our homeopathic coffee and went out to look.

"Across the way" was Buffalo's volunteer fire station, its scarlet and silver fire engines lined up outside the white doors of the single-story shed that usually housed them. One had a powerful circular badge on its door, a sturdy dog erect, its arms crossed, a yellow safety helmet on its head. EVER WILLING, EVER READY: FIREFIGHTERS it said.

A line of people passed through a small door and pushed donations into a box as three middle-aged women sat behind a table and counted not the money but the people.

"Six hundred and thirty so far," said the one in the middle, her hair died a subtle blond, her glasses giving an air of authority. Her fingers moved across a row of marks on her papers.

"That must be the whole population of Buffalo," I said. "Those old enough to walk, anyway."

She laughed as though the thought hadn't occurred to her.

"I guess it is."

"And who's thanking whom?"

"A bit of both. The firemen are doing something for the people of the town and the town loves its fire brigade." It was so American, so un-European.

Inside, the line gathered plastic trays and metal cutlery—even if it's plastic, cutlery is always referred to as "silverware"—and then passed a counter where well-built men in T-shirts were serving scrambled egg, circular sausage and two slices of pancake. We ate as firefighting overalls hung on hooks on the walls, heavy, soggy boots ready but wilting on the tiled floor. Metal doors the height of the building stood ready to unfurl should fire break out. Or they would have had the fire engines not been on the road already. I wondered what would happen to the pancake breakfast if I went outside and made a call.

Steph's neighbors at the table, unaware of my mischievous thoughts, were a couple who spent their winters in Florida and had seen much of Europe in 10 days. "We know it was a whirlwind but we got a taste of where we want to go back," said the short and stocky man with short dark hair, his face earnest and smiling at the same time, lined by having seen life a bit. She was one of those women you see looking for comfortable shoes in every shopping street in the world.

"We loved Luxembourg," she was saying. "It's really old, with genuine castles and villages, not like here, plus we saw it in the winter, in snow, and it was really cool." She meant the scenery rather than the weather.

They proclaimed France "beautiful" and everyone across Europe "real friendly."

"Even in Paris?"

"Well, yes, Paris… There was a coolness there."

We said even people in France don't think much of Parisians. Our neighbors were surprised and gratified.

"We want to do London, England," the man said, leaning across the table. He was bright-eyed, maybe in his late 60s. "We been there once."

"It was cool," his wife said.

"Next time, forget the Tube and get a street map and walk where you want to go," I suggested, "along the back streets. Then you'll see London is still just a collection of villages."

"And it's safe," Steph added.

"I was gonna ask you that," the man replied thoughtfully, relieved. He grew keen to get away, fidgeting as his wife pronounced a few other European cities and said they were cool, and then he concluded: "We realized over there what we'd been told, that your countries are like our states."

It wasn't long before we met the first riders coming the other way. We were, after all, hardly breaking fresh turf. We saw them coming slowly the other way, faint figures at first, then more distinguishable with their bags and that slow, syrupy progress that a loaded touring cyclist makes.

They were two middle-aged women, one on a recumbent, riding across America in stages. This time they'd get to their homes in Ohio before setting off again for the Atlantic. Then a couple of lone riders. And almost every one said: "Sam's ahead of you."

"Who's Sam?"

"French, we think. And he's feeling lonely because he's ridden all the way from Maine and he hasn't come across anyone to ride with."

"Poor guy."

"Yes, nice guy, too. Fairly young. But lonely."

Day after day passed with news of Sam. Sometimes he was French, other times British. Sometimes he was two days ahead, other times three. But always just ahead on the road. Lois hadn't mentioned him at Monroeville, so perhaps he'd just ridden through. He was becoming the mystery man of the ride.

We hoped he was enjoying the generosity, friendship and warmth of Americans that we were experiencing. Time and again we have been left breathless by the way strangers have helped us.

JUNE

America is the only country that went from barbarism to decadence without civilization in between.

—*Oscar Wilde*

3

Do you recall a former life, living in Atlantis, but don't care to tell anyone? Talking about it with others making you uneasy?

Ashkum stood at the end of a windy and weary ride over open countryside. The spirit was willing but the flesh was weak. We plodded with the wind blowing in the opposite direction—until now we have been blessed by tailwinds—and Steph hid on my wheel. We got slower and slower as one slight rise after another turned into an Alp. And then, at last, the water tower we'd seen from an hour away announced we were there.

In parts of Britain, you navigate by church steeples. Here, it's water towers. They have a regional style. In some parts they look like Sputnik, although far larger, giant round tanks, sometimes square tanks, standing on frail and splaying legs. The fashion in Indiana is to build them like golf balls standing on a spindly tee. They stand, tempting, deceiving, as distant objectives. Sometimes, too, there are grain silos, metallic cathedrals of the plain, ugly but welcoming for the promise of shelter, food and drink their community provides.

In Ashkum, the water tower is painted with the town's name and, beneath it, black cutouts of a man and woman holding hands. Imagine the shape you'd cut in folded newspaper to make a paper chain and you get the idea. It's only a tiny place, Ashkum, on the railway but bypassed by an interstate. There were fewer than 60 people eligible to vote when the town was founded in 1856 and there are only 750 now. They lead a quiet life watching crops grow all around them.

Like many towns in middle America, Ashkum allowed travelers to camp in the park. There were two parks and, typical of the friendship of Americans, a driver stopped as we rode towards the first to tell us we ought to be heading for the second. That was where we could pitch our tent. But we ought to find the village policeman to be sure the showers would be open. Life is so quiet that the police ensure passing cyclists get a good wash.

We couldn't find the policeman and we didn't like to bother the mayor. Making the logical decision that if you can't find one person in uniform then another will do, we went to the fire station. And there, in the absence of anything smoldering, they set to work to find the missing *flic*. In time, he turned up, a mean hombre in dark glasses, leaning on the door post without speaking. He all but chewed on a matchstick. He had a gun in his pocket but he didn't look pleased to see us.

"You guys wanna follow me?" he asked grumpily in that way that turned an invitation into a command. He got into a white patrol car painted in gold and black and surmounted by as much rooftop paraphernalia as you'd find on a battleship. American policemen don't stint themselves when it comes to the glorious. We rode wearily behind him through suburban streets, round three sides of a square and eventually to the park. We were thirsty, very thirsty, and hungry.

"Most cyclists set up just about there," the policeman said, his car parked with its door open at the roadside. He waved at an area away from the pavilion and its bright lights. "The mayor'll be along in ten minutes to open up for you." We asked his opinion on cold beers and food, thanked him for his trouble, and he walked away with his gun on his hip. Moments later he was back.

"Course, the other option is that you come home and stay with us," he said. "You could have a soft bed and drink a beer with us. And we can launder all your dirty clothes if you want."

No tired cyclist could object to anything in that list. Especially with storms forecast. Amazed once more at the spontaneous friendliness and generosity of Americans, we said we'd be there as soon as a cold beer and tired legs would allow.

"I used to be an avid cyclist," Jim said. "I've ridden four double centuries..." He shrugged. "Now all I do is talk about it."

He and Kathy lived four miles south. They had four boisterous and agile dogs, three of which Kathy trains for agility competitions. The fourth is too old. In the backyard was an obstacle course of white hurdles with blue and red stripes. Jim, off-duty, is not the man we met on the road. He is gentle, wears glasses rather than *hombre* shades, and has less hair than I do. A minute telephone clipped to his ear would alert him if society needed him to fight for truth, justice and the American way.

Not that he has to much. He doesn't carry a gun off duty. "Other policemen think that's nonsense, because this is a job where you could meet someone you put in jail, which is why city policemen stick together and drink in the same bars, but out here I don't see a risk. "I haven't put anyone in jail for ten years and pretty much nothing happens in town, and that's the way people like it. There are a couple of bars in town and sometimes there's a disturbance there, but that's about it." He spoke of a colleague who saw things differently: he left his gun at home when he went to church, thinking it inappropriate—a gunman came in and started firing.

Jim worked 30 hours a week, usually in the evening into the small hours, picking his own hours. The state police are on the edge of town but townspeople like their own cop on the street at night. The rest of the time he worked either for a local farmer whom he believes employs him more for his company than for any agricultural contribution, or for a security agency near Chicago, where everyone assumes he's a tough city cop—"And Chicago cops are pretty tough, believe me"—and give him no trouble. Most of the other guards are moonlighting policemen from the big city. "I sit outside buildings for which the owner pays for security and nobody bothers me because they think I'm a Chicago cop and nobody messes with a Chicago cop."

He was 62 and he'd been in the police for decades, and in a lot of different towns. Kathy worked for UPS, the parcel service. When UPS moves her to a new base, Jim moves with her, to another force. His spare room had a 1970s bike on an equally old turbo, a sweat towel on the handlebars. There were pictures of Lance Armstrong in the kitchen and a sparkling road bike in the hall, "paid for by an insurance company after I was knocked off my other bike by an old lady who really shouldn't have been driving."

Kathy's advice in the morning is that we ought to pass through Stelle.

"They built a spaceship there," she said invitingly, "and they're still hoping to fly off in it." She hesitated. "Or is it that they're *expecting* a spaceship? Anyway, our messengers say it's an odd place and they're not allowed in. They have to leave parcels at a checkpoint."

Léo Woodland

You can't help but feel fond of people who have built their own spaceship and so we set off to look. Stelle was just off our route, in the middle of flat, open and windy countryside. It would be easy to see a spacecraft. Sadly, we saw nothing. When we got there, the place looked like an upmarket housing estate, with a name board set in flowers at the entrance, speed bumps to deter over-enthusiastic Martian drivers, and cars parked outside generous houses. We heard a goat, it's true, and we saw a wind pump, but what's that set against whooshing off into the clouds?

It took a while to unravel the story. It seems a man called Richard Kieninger, who spent too much time in California and came to believe that he had been guided by an ancient and secretive organization called The Brotherhoods, believed something awful was about to happen to Earth. He must have been persuasive because in plenty of time for 2000, when whatever was going to happen was going to happen, he led followers to a land he called Stelle and there they built 25 homes, a school and a sewage treatment plant. Plus what were mysteriously called "underground facilities." He'd hoped for 250,000 people by the turn of the century but that was to be only the first of his disappointments. Another was that the world didn't come to an end.

Even if it had, Kieninger wouldn't have been at Stelle to see it happen. It was the mid-1970s when he and his followers built the place and that entailed a lot of hanging about. His followers occupied themselves with building, with a plastics factory and even making pianos. Kieninger busied himself seducing a great many of the women, causing enough upset that he had to clear off and start another community in Texas. The business about the spaceship seems to have been local invention, although I like to think it was true.

The faith is kept down the road in Kempton, though. It's an odd place. Ride through on the main highway and you'd notice nothing. Turn off a block and you enter a land of murals, of Sergeant Pepper and desert travel and a whole building covered in discontent-looking newts. A ventilator hatch has been transformed into a hot air balloon creeping up a wall and a verandah has become a sort of Indian reservation with totem poles.

Across the road from Sergeant Pepper—were there cowboys, bikini girls and the Blues Brothers in the original?—is the desert scene, all pyramids and a sphinx. It's on the wall of *Adventures Unlimited*, a new-age-and-conspiracy bookshop outside which stood a scaled-down version of the statues on Easter Island. Inside was free coffee, although we didn't realize at the time that it was a gift, which left us feeling ashamed to have asked for something fresher.

Adventures Unlimited is a magazine and a mail-order business. Its 64-page catalogue offers "UFOs, Atlantis, Templars, Lost Cities, Anti-Gravity, Ancient Science, Street Societies, Tesla Technology and Much More." No fewer than 624 pages of *Gravitational Manipulation of Domed Craft* reveal—for the first time—"the scientific principles behind UFO propulsion mechanics and shows that these principles are known and recognized by today's scientists."

Another book, 324 pages, tempts buyers: "Near where the sunken warships of the Battle of Guadalcanal lie, glowing UFOs rise out of the Pacific, fly into the mountains and disappear into jungle lakes. Here, a tropical paradise exists with inexplicable, ancient ruins and puzzling writings of an unknown culture."

The magazine cover shows a flying saucer with rocket ships landing and others whizzing out of portholes. It costs "$6 USD, $5 Euro [*sic*], 7 Darians." It offers "Strange Tales of Discovery and More Far-Out Adventures in Far Away Places." The articles were seriously written, mainly by David Hatcher Childress, a follower of the Stelle guru. Stelle, by the way, has long disassociated itself with its wacky past.

"News from around the world" told us that a British man, unemployed and 55, had unearthed the greatest Anglo-Saxon hoard on record. Two Italians thought they had found what's left of an army of 50,000 that Cambyses, son of Cyrus the Great, sent to cause trouble in Egypt in 525BCE. But it's the classified ads that provide the real entertainment. One asked

> ARE YOU PART of the Time Travel class action lawsuit stuck in the 2007-2014 time glitch? The claimants against the makers of the SA-989 series of Polywarp Time Machines sold until the recall of 2024 will meet at...

A joke, presumably, although with people like that it's not simple to tell. I thought this one is serious, though:

> DO YOU RECALL a former life, living in Atlantis, but don't care to tell anyone? Talking about it with others making you uneasy? Contact...

Léo Woodland

I enjoyed the ad inviting me to send someone $6 for information on how to become a millionaire. I wasn't sure about the warning that "Alien Talk Show hosts walk among us" and I didn't feel ready to

> DISCOVER the sensual beauty of unassisted homebirth. Read inspiring birth stories and articles, view stunning pregnancy, birth and breastfeeding photos, and purchase unassisted homebirth books and videos. Bornfree! The Unassisted Childbirth Page...

But it all made up for an otherwise dull ride to Odell.

Odell would be nothing were it not for Jim Rebholz and Route 66. Jim is vice-president of the Odell Bank, which in reality is a branch of the Pontiac Bank that kept its name to please regulars. He was a smiling, round-faced man who cuts the grass in the park. "Some guys play golf and I do this," he said. In the winter he coaches basketball. We told him we already knew his name, that wondrous words were said about him, his town and its welcome for cyclists. He smiled shyly and said he would have to look himself up. He made us welcome, brought a box of beers and opened the park's white shed in case we wanted to sleep there. We did, spreading our bags on tables laid on the cement floor.

"We get about a dozen cyclists a year pass through," he said as we sat round a bench between the shed and the swings. "Never met a bad one yet. You're all great guys."

I asked about his work. My father was a postman, I said, and reckoned there wasn't much about life on his round that he couldn't deduce from the letters he delivered. "Can't do that about someone's life in a bank," he said. "A mailman, he sees where all the mail comes from. He can guess things from that. There just isn't time in a bank to go through who's paying what to whom."

Odell now is commuter-land. There were farms all around but mostly people traveled to Pontiac. Once they traveled from elsewhere to Odell, so many that their cars were bumper to bumper through town. It was so busy that a tunnel was built in 1934 for villagers to cross the road. The drivers didn't want to be in Odell, of course. They wanted to get through it. Odell was on Route 66.

Just the name breathes glamor and romance. The first time I came across it was on a Rolling Stones record. I loved the list of names, although I couldn't understand the way Mick Jagger pronounced them. I especially liked "Down through Winona... Flagstaff, Arizona." I had no idea where they or anywhere else was. I found out later that Bob Troup, who wrote the song, hadn't intended to make it a gazetteer at all. He just couldn't think of anything else to write and listed a load of towns. Even Americans couldn't place Winona, which Troup included because nowhere else rhymed with "Flagstaff, Arizona." It's not even in the right place geographically.

Route 66 ran from Chicago to Los Angeles. It was the road taken by those ruined by the Dust Bowl years of the 1930s and then, in happier times, by sun-seekers heading for California. I'd always wondered if there was a Route 65 or a Route 67. It turns out there were. Still are. Route 65 connects the north and south of middle western America; route 67 starts in about the same place and also travels south but veers off then into Texas.

Route 66 was going to be Route 60, an equally valid number but rejected after arguments because it wasn't as euphonious as 66. The road changed over the years, bypassing Odell to the west rather than running through its center, and it vanished from the map in 1985. It fell victim to the interstate network, as did Odell because traffic now hurries past as a distant roar. It makes the town more pleasant but no longer are there countless business along its route.

Most of those businesses in Odell, were gas stations. There were ten of them. You could bowl a hoop from one to the next. When Route 66 was born in 1926, almost 80 percent of the world's cars were in America: one for every five people, compared to 33 in France and 6,130 in Russia. You bought your fuel in unlabelled cans from general stores. Shopkeepers stopped taking fuel to houses when a lot of deliveries ended in explosions.

The first drive-in gas station, in St. Louis, was a tin shack with a converted water tank on stilts draining fuel to cars. It was pointed out to the editor of a trade magazine with the words "Get a good laugh out of this dump." But by 1929 there were 143,000 of them. East of the Rockies back then they were called "service stations"; to the west, "filling stations." One of them still stands in Odell and it's a place of pilgrimage from all over.

We rode from Jim's park and along the broad and deserted road that was Route 66. Neat, single-story houses stood back behind roadside verges and then open gardens. The old subway for villagers was still there, with a sign giving its history, but it had been cemented closed in 1947. An old Mobil station still stood, two bays and a modern pump but decayed and peeling. The forecourt was bare and puddled by rain but inside the workshop were old cars in the course of restoration.

Along the road a little further, someone had assembled a garden museum of garage artifacts: red fuel pumps, an oil drum, work stands and general clutter of an age past. And then, on the very outskirts, the gas station that has become, literally, a national treasure. It's on the national register of historic places. It tells of a different era. The tourist people say: "It was the habit of Bob Close [the owner] to go into downtown Odell for lunch every day. He left the pumps on while he was gone. If a customer came by and needed gas, he/she would pump it themselves and write down on the side of the gas pump their name and how much they owed. Later in the week they would drop by, pay the bill, and wipe their name of the pump.

"This seemed to be a very good system which allowed Bob to get a hot meal and his customers to get the fuel they needed. At least it was until that fateful day when the Sinclair representative [Bob has switched to Sinclair gasoline] stopped by at lunch time. He saw the 'Gone to Lunch' sign on the door and decided to wait.

"While he was waiting, he saw what looked to him like someone had been doodling on the side of the gas pump. 'We can't have that,' he thought to himself. So he decided that he would help Bob out. He got a rag and a spray bottle of cleaning solution from the trunk of his car that he carried for just this type of occasion. It was clean as a whistle when he was through. Bob didn't lose a dime. When folks heard what had happened, they came in and settled their debt. That is just the way it was back then."

The first filling stations had their pumps by the road. Traffic grew. Lines of cars backed up when anyone used the pumps. There wasn't room to pass. The station in Odell was more modern: the pumps were set back from the road as we'd expect now. This particular one was built in 1932, although the house-and-canopy style was one that Standard Oil had used since 1916. Odell bought it in 1999.

It stood like a little house, white with blue trimming, the walls in white brick cleaner than ever they must have been in the past. "Standard Oil Co" was printed across the angled roof in darker tiles.

There were bright red advertisements for Miller Tires running down the canopy pillars and a dark blue horizontal one on the front wall of the building for "Standard Oil Products." A hanging white sign boasted "Clean Bathrooms." There was a single red pump, a tall slender conical affair topped by a transparent drum through which the gas must have passed. The whole was topped, about 12 feet high, by an incongruous white plastic crown of the sort you'd see in the Tower of London. Press a button and an affectionate voice explained you were treading where American history was written.

"We get people from all over America to see it," Jim Rebholz told us, "even from Europe." Such is the legend of Route 66. Enough that someone has placed Route 66 shields on trees beside it. But they and the garage are all that remain of the Mother Road.

Indiana was kind to us but it rarely thrilled. Like Ohio, it was full of friendly people and small towns. But it was an agricultural industrial estate. Hour after hour passed as a green desert of maize and soy—the wheat vanished after a while—without anything but a rare slope to relieve suffering bottoms. When we approached Cambridge on a road which finally tossed up and down like a food-poisoned stomach, we complained, of course...

Illinois led me to win a bet with an American by knowing that the state capital was Springfield and not the more logical Chicago, as she insisted. A hundred Belgian francs was worth about $1.50 so her honor and my conceit came pretty cheap.

People in Illinois are proud of their state. Time and again we were asked how we found it, with the desired answer obvious in their enthusiasm. This was rich farming country, some of the richest in the country, with land prices to match according to farmers we spoke to. But the roads were awful. The surface itself was fine. There were few potholes. But Illinois knows no other way to make highways than to lay slabs of something hard and then seal the gaps with tar. The idea was that the road can expand and contract with the weather. The reality was that the filling of tar compressed into ridges or drops into holes. In a car you'd notice nothing more than a frop-frop-frop beneath your wheels. On a bike you notice far more: you notice that every four turns of the pedals the bike bumps beneath you, shaking your arms, beating your bottom and shaking your brain.

Léo Woodland

We came to dread or look forward to county boundaries. American counties are small, just glorified parishes. Each county, as well as having its own police force, surfaces its own roads. America is not a country where people willingly pay taxes to the public good and so the job is often done in the least expensive way. The generosity of counties and their concern for the well-being of those who passed through became an important part of our day. We moved alternately between ridable and miserable roads. It's hard to think kindly of a state, however pretty, however friendly, when it shakes the fillings from your teeth.

There were diversions, incidental entertainment laid on for our pleasure. Who would have thought, for instance, that the Union Federal Bank in Kewanee would have otters on its banking floor? Or, more precisely, one otter because the other one died a few months before we got there. The pool with its rocks and streams took up two floors in the middle of the bank. White signs printed in black, mourning, capitals were fixed to its edge.

"Gone but not forgotten" said one. Alongside was another. "Oscar, died December 23, 2008." And alongside that a picture of Oscar staring at the camera, ears raised and looking like a rabbit in the moment before it's hit by a truck. He was 20 when he died. That left just Andy, a year younger, who must now be pondering his own mortality. He's a bit stiffer than he was, it seemed, and he sleeps more than he did, but he splashed happily enough to amuse us.

We walked into the bank in the center of town and said shyly that we had no money to open an account but that we wouldn't mind seeing, as we thought at the time, the two otters. A young clerk sitting at an open table said "Well, of course." Life in banking was undemanding at that moment because within seconds we had been joined by two other clerks. They gestured to a big hole, filled with water and lit from beneath, further into the building. "I'll see if I can find you somebody to tell you more," one said.

The somebody turned out to be the vice-president, Thomas Martineau, a balding, middle-aged man in a white shirt, dark pants and a discreet spotted tie. Talking to foreigners about otters was clearly making his afternoon more pleasant.

"You're in luck because Andy's out swimming," he said. "There's a tunnel from his tank down to a lower level so that people can see him from the street. But we had to put a little gate in because he used to stop halfway down the tunnel and when people come in here to see him and he's not here, we say he must be down by the pavement and they go down there and he's not there either and he's stopped in the pipe.

"We got the otters from Louisiana back in 1991. A former president was fascinated by otters and when the bank was extended and he decided to have a central feature, he said he'd acquire a couple of otters. People come from all over to see them, which is strange because we do nothing to promote that they're here, but you're the first people we've seen from France."

Thomas spoke quickly and nervously, one of those people so keen to tell you shyly of their enthusiasm that he didn't quite take in what was said to him in return. Determined not to get on with his work, he took us on a long guided tour of the underneath of the bank where Andy spends the night in a wire cages and eats "the same meat they feed to lions and tigers in circuses, plus smelts".

When Oscar died just before Christmas Day there was a big piece in the paper but no town funeral. The bank decided not to replace him and nobody's decided what to do when Andy dies.

Kewanee was big compared to other towns we've been in. It called itself the hog capital of the world and made its point by having half a pig sticking out of a wall. "Then someone hitched it to the back of his car and drove off down the road with it," a cafe owner told us during a Sticky Bun Opportunity. "Ain't so many *haaagz* as there was either. Most are over on the other side of town, the way you're going, but they ain't so many these days."

Reaching the Mississippi was as much a landmark as greeting Route 66. It came after a wet night in a campsite outside Cambridge. It poured when we got to the village and it fell again as the light dwindled, flooding grass and earth alike. The tent was secure. It has withstood terrifying blasts at the peak of the Pyrenees, when the valleys all around were filled by cloud like a gray sea, and it has stayed dry in Wagnerian rain in eastern Europe. But that didn't stop us feeling aggrieved at having to run the 50 yards to the tent from the shelter where we cooked and ate.

It rained again in the morning and it rained until noon. We splashed back through Cambridge and on to Orion, pronounced OR-ree-on, for coffee. Coffee is sold everywhere in America. In cafés it is just about strong enough to taste of something, and it is refilled over and over without extra charge, but in gas stations it is so weak that you can all but see the bottom of the mug. We'd have been happy with anything at that moment. The problem was finding it. People don't walk in the streets in America. They come out of their houses, get into their cars, and drive off. Asking directions is therefore not easy. The British writer, Josie Dew, was speaking of Los Angeles, which is an extreme case, but the principles hold true elsewhere. She wrote:

"There was none of the sense of community which is found in any European town or city. You couldn't trot down to a corner shop to pick up a paper or a pint of milk or swap a bit of gossip with the locals—the nearest shops were a car ride away in the mall along a dangerously traffic-laden highway. You couldn't nip round the corner to post a letter because there were no post boxes—the mall was all or nothing. Nor did people pass the time of day on street corners or cross the road to greet friends, any more than people in Britain chat on the M1/M25 intersection [the M1 is the main motorway or interstate north from London and the M25 the city's ring road]. It's not that this lack of street life is necessarily wrong: it's just different and strangely sad."

Find someone, though, and the help as ever is overpowering. Nobody is more friendly than an American asked for assistance. We eventually marooned a man between his car and his house, we in waterproofs and he standing in drizzle in a checkered shirt.

"*Higher Dawn?*," he asked as we wheeled up, miserable examples of human life wrapped in bright yellow. We said we were doing fine, given the circumstances, but that coffee and Sticky Buns would improve the situation enormously.

"*Waaahl*," he said as he thought. "The only place you could *walk* in would be Subway, I guess." Subway is an omnipresent chain which sells sandwiches which don't quite taste of much. "You'd have to go a couple of blocks over to the hard road."

There were two interesting points here. The first and less significant was the reference to the "hard road", which must have been the name that stuck when it was the first road through town to be surfaced. It could have been within living memory for some. Hard to remember now that America that had barely any hard-surfaced roads at all at the start of the 20th century. Indeed, in 1919 a young soldier called Dwight Eisenhower was about to leave the army when he got the chance to join a motorized expedition "through darkest America with truck and tank," as he called it. There were 42 trucks, motorcycles, cars, ambulance, repair teams, field kitchens and searchlight teams. Read those last two words again: they give an idea of what it meant to drive in the USA in just the last century.

The convoy left Washington on July 7, 1919, and for three days managed a shade more than five and a half miles a day. Axles broke, tires bogged into nonexistent roads. It didn't reach San Francisco until September 6. The idea had been to see how long the army would take to reach the Pacific if Japan invaded. The answer, clearly, was quite a long time. The term "highway" still meant no more than a way higher and therefore dryer than the bogs and deserts through which it passed.

The other point in the man-in-the-checkered-shirt's comment was that Subway was the only place in town you could *walk* into. He turned out to be wrong but the point remains that he was hard-pressed to think of anywhere that wasn't a drive-in. You can drive in almost everything and everywhere in America. Buy pizzas or burgers, buy medicines, withdraw money from your bank… You can do it all without getting out of your car. Except buy gas.

It rained, too, when we reached the Mississippi and crossed into Iowa. Or, at any rate, the bridge into Muscatine was set against a drop of angry black and the wind blew in that way that said "I'm going to tip down on you any time now." We found the cheapest place in town, perhaps unwisely named the Muskie Motel, and holed up for two nights.

Mark Twain used to work in Muscatine. He worked for the local paper before he became famous, when he was still Sam Clemens. He wrote: "I remember Muscatine for its summer sunsets. I have never seen any, on either side of the ocean, that equaled them. They used the broad smooth river as a canvas, and painted on it every imaginable dream of color, from the mottled daintiness and delicacies of the opal, all the way up, through cumulative intensities, to blinding purple and crimson conflagrations which were enchanting to the eye, but sharply tried it at the same time.

"All the Upper Mississippi region has these extraordinary sunsets as a familiar spectacle. It is the true Sunset Land: I am sure no other country can show so good a right to the name. The sunrises are also said to be exceedingly fine. I do not know." His other memory of the town is that a lunatic said he'd kill him if he didn't agree that he was the only son of Satan. I have no idea if Twain agreed but in similar circumstances I think I would have done.

The comments about the sunsets used to be engraved overlooking the river at the sadly named Mark Twain Overlook. It's an unappealing triangle of grass and a single flagpole overlooking the river, the bridge and a shedlike factory that obscures most of the finer parts of town. Everything is chained to the ground. It was less than a cultural treat. Mark Twain would have left town. Instead, his words have left town, or at any rate have left the view of the factory, because the council grew tired of the way it was vandalized.

The only advantages to being up there were, first, to notice how much the flag of Iowa resembles the flag of France, and second, to see that a bike path ran along the bank of the Mississippi. The river no longer has the mud bank romance of America's greatest river and the era in which Twain placed Huckleberry Finn had vanished two decades before he invented him. I must read Huck Finn again. I tried it when I was nine or ten, any tale of a young boy wading barefoot in mud and getting into trouble being of appeal at that age, but I didn't get on with it. Twain wrote it in the first person, in Finn's words, and used expressions and dialects little used in the public-housing areas of north London where I lived. We had a way of talking of our own and, while getting muddy in the pond in the park had at least some similarities with Huck, little of the rest did. I must have another go.

Muscatine used to have the largest black population in Iowa, into which the windblown bridge brought us. Slaves and free blacks alike fled across the river from further east. The story of slavery in America had been with us since we finished with the Adirondacks and began flirting with the Lakes and the Canadian border. It was there that the Underground Railway came to life for us. The first time was in Pultneyville, an expensive village in New York where French "batteaux men" (people couldn't spell then) stopped by in 1687 to trade with local Indians. They did no more than buy, sell and move on, however, and the first white settler was a hunter called Yankee Bill Waters. But that wasn't until 1804. He would have been familiar even then with slavery.

So was Samuel Cuyler. Just back from where the "batteaux men" landed stood a blue and gold board before a splendid white house set back from the road by an airport of grass. It marked where Cuyler hid escaped slaves before passing them to Canada and freedom. America had a spot of bother over keeping slaves and North and South came to see things differently. Some in the South, though, sided with the slaves. Escape routes began not long after Yankee Bill set up beside Lake Ontario. More than 30,000 escaped into Canada in the 50 years that followed.

I knew little about the Underground Railroad. And it became a reality only when we stopped—with some emotion, I admit—at this first and unexpected sign. It wasn't a railroad and it was underground only in that it was secret. The name came from the way slaves passed from station to station, one hiding place to the next. Similarities to a railroad brought words to go with it. Conductors led individuals or small groups up to 20 miles a night, sometimes walking, sometimes in a wagon. Conductors could be freeborn blacks, white abolitionists, former slaves or Indians but no one knew more than his own part in the whole scheme. Rest points became stations. Those who gave money or clothing were stockholders.

The number who escaped was lower than the natural increase in the population. To this day nobody knows how many succeeded. But the psychological impact was enormous and Southern newspapers offered rewards for escaped slaves. Federal marshals and bounty hunters set off in chase. Being a free black wasn't safe either because strong, healthy blacks were valuable and it wasn't unusual for them to be kidnapped. The Fugitive Slave Law denied suspected fugitives a jury and they couldn't testify; the marshal or slavecatcher had only to swear an oath to acquire a writ for return of property. Judges were paid $10 to force a suspected slave back to slavery, $5 to free him.

Muscatine, or at any rate a barber in town, welcomed fleeing slaves. Alexander Clark helped them escape, organized petitions to overturn racist laws, and in 1863 helped organize Iowa's black regiment, the 60th United States Colored Infantry. In a premature nod to the current habit of referring to black people as African Americans, it was originally the 1st Iowa Infantry, African Descent. Five years later, in 1868, he sued the school that turned away his daughter because she was black. The case desegregated Iowa's public schools. His son, also called Alexander, was the first black graduate of the University of Iowa College of Law. And his father, at 58, became ambassador to Liberia. Not bad, eh?

Muscatine makes nothing of its history in improving the life of black people. Nothing we saw, anyway. Instead, it clings to a past in which it made the world's buttons, shaped from mussel shells scooped from the river by long-handled spoons. "Still make buttons here," said a rotund gent who said he rode a bike and wore a cycling T-shirt, "but they're plastic these days." He and his overweight wife tucked into Sticky Buns and stirred sugar into their coffee. They kept naming local cyclists and asking if we knew them. A steady procession of *leezure* riders moved up and down the bike path. It ran from a big park which holds a hilly bike race every summer down to the drinks factory that stood on a bend in the river and used much of the grain we saw pushed in barges along the river.

Muscatine still has factories—furniture, drink—but nothing of the romance of pearl. It's a long way from when the town made four of every ten pearl buttons in the world, when 45 factories turned out close to half the world's production, one and a half million of them a year. There was a button display at the tourist office—button presses, old posters—but tourists might be in town at weekends so on Sunday it's shut. A giant sculpture of a pearl-fisher on the river bank stood in accidental symbolism with its back to the water.

We left Muscatine on a mission: to visit the world's oldest soda-jerk. At 90, he has little reason to expect a challenge. He's worked at the Candy Kitchen since he was six and he's still there now, his white shirt neat, his bow tie in place, his smile a slow, world-warming grin that opens across his face. He looks 15 years younger, but then "when your life has always been just to make people happy, you never grow old."

The Candy Kitchen is in the heart of Wilton, a town which shouldn't be judged by its hideous outskirts of tire depots, fast-food joints and all the other social detritus which ruins the edge of so many American towns. Turn off from all that and ride down the slope into town and you enter an older, more gentle town. A town that befits George Nopoulos. The outside was brick, three stories high, the uppermost blank, the middle graced with three tall and elegant windows and a less elegant sign that points with an arrow carrying the word SODA. And then beneath a striped red and white awning, the red fascia with blinds that incongruously say "Ye ol' ice cream parlor" on the left and "founded in 1860 by R. A. McIntire" on the right. In America, 1860 is plenty old enough to have the Middle Ages styling of "ye".

Inside were walnut booths fitted in marble and glass and mirrors. Each had its own leaded glass lamp shade. In a back room were old golden cash registers and the slab on which Gus Nopoulos made ice cream from 1910 to 1946. When we walked in, George was serving a gaggle of six-year-olds. Their parents stood behind them as the children sat untidily on the row of scarlet stools and asked question after question about the ice cream, and its flavors, that George makes on the premises.

"Oh, I don't know," he replied in mock tired frustration to a girl with long blond hair pulled back with a ribbon. "I only started here last week." That smile, that favorite-uncle smile, spread over his face.

The building in which the Candy Kitchen stands was built seven years before a struggling Illinois lawyer wrote the Gettysburg Address. It went up a year after the Mississippi and Missouri Railroad spread this far in 1855, giving birth to a town named, as it happens, after a town far to the east in Maine. Wilton had a sweet tooth from the start and R. A. McIntire prospered in the ice cream parlor he opened in 1860, a year before the Civil War.

McIntire had no reason to know that among thousands of immigrants at Ellis Island in 1907 was young Gus George Chimpanis, all of 5 feet 4 inches tall. He was 16 and his mother had sewn $25 into his coat. It was all he had apart from the address of the uncle in Davenport, Iowa, who had paid his fare. Uncle John was also in the candy and ice cream business and Gus celebrated three years there by becoming American and changing his name to Nopoulous. He is said to be the inventor of the banana split, a creation that came from a glut of bananas. Gus cut them in half and nestled the slice around the ice cream.

We're far enough back now that the President was William Taft, women couldn't vote and the Wright Brothers were pestering the army to buy their first airplane. He and a friend went to the fair in Wilton Junction. McIntire had retired and the two passed his closed shop. The interior was intact. Gus bought it and took $17 on the first day, two months' rent. The next day, a Sunday, he took $25. The parlor stayed open 365 days a year for the next century. Three generations have worked there. George started at six, in 1926. His job: to stand on a chair and keep the Brunswick record player wound. Thelma started almost as young, washing dishes when she was 10. They married in 1949, after George gave her an engagement ring in the back room of the Candy Kitchen.

Léo Woodland

He told us his story as he must have told it to thousands, but without any sign that we weren't the first. He looked over his shoulder and added an extra scoop of ice cream to my plate with a finger-on-lips gesture that said "Don't tell Thelma."

"Another few years and he'll have got the job off pat," Thelma said without looking round.

"They tell me I've qualified to retire," George said. The joke is that he provides a Pensioners' Special for "old folk" two decades younger than he is. He still starts work at six every morning.

"And will you retire?"

"Can't see why when I'm enjoying myself so much."

"Your sons aren't interested in taking over?"

"They don't wanna get mixed up in all this. Heck, I leave the keys in the door all day and still people refuse to come in and take over!"

We felt better after our first real day off. We'd been filling our breaks instead of relaxing. It was a treat to take the train to Chicago, for instance, even though it rained and we were the only tourists on the tour boat. We fell in love with the winding river, its steely, glass-fronted skyscrapers and, smaller among them, the original brick buildings that so impressed the world when they reached for the sky. It was here that "skyscraper" was coined in 1885.

This is the city the world associates with gangsters and one entrepreneur built a block into which rich residents could drive rather than be mugged on the street. On the top floor of this Jewelers Building, without anyone knowing, lived a short fleshy man who said he was in the furniture business. Everyone else knew him as Al Capone.

American trains were once glamorous. Streamlined locomotives hissing steam and bristling with bells and lanterns hauled businessmen and fur-clad ladies the width of the country in trains with names like Broadway Limited and Twentieth Century. Then the car—Eisenhower dreamed of an interstate road network after his haul to the Pacific—and the plane and the American fondness for speed and convenience over quality, plus a still more marked reluctance to spend private money for the public good… they all killed the great expresses.

There are still good passenger trains in America, run by a national network called Amtrak, but they use lines hired from freight-train companies. The rails are chipped and uneven. Speeds are kept down for safety and down again because a passenger train at 60 mph needs a lot of 30 mph freight trains to stop to let it pass on a single-line track. And most American railways are single line.

Amtrak does its best, though. Critics insist you'll arrive three days late, assuming you haven't been held up along the way by masked men riding ponies. But those who told the worst stories had traveled the trains least. Amtrak's daily Cardinal from New York to Chicago was never fast and only a devotee would take it the whole way because it dives down through Philadelphia and Washington, but it is pleasant, relaxed and comfortable. We arrived not three days late but several minutes early, having drunk coffee, chatted with staff and followed the journey in a folding pamphlet. The trouble was that excursions like that could be as tiring as the bike riding they replaced. In Muscatine we strolled a little and we slept a lot. It worked wonders.

The riding became hillier. Only a cyclist would understand why that could be good news. Shallow valleys showed off the different shades of green crops. Trees clustered beside the road to watch us pass, shaking their arms gently to wish us *bonne route*. The air became fresh and beautiful. Life had started looking better. We camped beside a baseball pitch on the edge of Oxford Junction, a crossroads where the town hall was in an old and tiny wooden gas station that still had its lone pump. Locals spoke of a thunderstorm but by dusk there was no sign. People always warn of storms in America; it is a national obsession.

A small road trailed beside the park and we watched the occasional car pass and the occasional cow look up from its grazing to watch. For the first time, perhaps because we have crossed the Mississippi and our route will now take us north to the river's source and on to the Canadian border, we felt we were in Middle America. We have passed into the "square" states. Every state west of the Mississippi—except for Oregon, Minnesota and Texas—has at least two straight or nearly straight sides. Colorado and Wyoming are rectangular. It was Thomas Jefferson's idea when America began imposing the dull grid pattern that typifies everywhere but its oldest towns. Roads are numbered from a central point, the first north 1 North, the first south 1 South and so on. It took a while to realize that Route 32W, say, was a long way from Route 32E and not simply the same road in the opposite direction.

Jefferson's world was flat, like a map. The real world curved in all directions. So while he could ignore the rivers and mountains that more pleasantly and logically constitute borders elsewhere, he was foiled by the curve of the earth. He had to make his north-south roads jump to one side every 24 miles. So if you ride them now, you go in a straight line for an hour and a half and then, when you reach a road going east-west, take a staggered junction so the world can once more match Jefferson's wishes.

Out-of-town towns with no name grew up where larger roads crossed one of Eisenhower's interstates, places with no connection to anywhere except the distant destinations on their signposts. Still less do they have connection with reality. They are a strange, detached world of Kentucky Fried Chickens and McDonalds, where nobody lives, where everything is in primary colors lit by neon. They cater to those too tired to drive or to care where they are. They exist only in America and you tell them by the fixed smiles on the staff and the haggard looks on everyone else.

We rode on to Dyersville and it rained all day. On the good side, the wind blew so hard that even the birds started walking. And it blew from behind us. That was the good side. The bad side was that we were shaken by 35,000 expansion joints or cracks. That's Steph's calculation of one every two meters and therefore 500 for every kilometer multiplied by the 70 kilometers we rode the main highway because bridge construction forced us off the back roads. It was a road of Soviet standards, worse even than in Illinois, and we trust Iowa is ashamed of it. Or perhaps it isn't. They have a habit of getting things wrong round here. The center of Dyersville has a magnificent basilica with 64 stained glass windows. One is more remarkable than the others. The instructions for the job were to show St Francis Xavier ministering to Indians. I suppose that's all it said. The glass man looked at the sheet and drew Red Indians. Only too late did he realize they were supposed to be Indians from India.

We looked around the church once the rain had stopped and we had wrung out our clothes in a hotel and rinsed them of road grit. We wheeled our bikes through a back door and left winding snakes of dirt along the carpet. It didn't matter that it rained. Some days it does, most days it doesn't. The road bumps, though, will live with us for ages.

We wouldn't complain about the hills today, either. Views are often proportional to the three dimensional qualities of the land. Iowa had been a state unlike any other since Pennsylvania. It is Irish green, dotted as has been much of our route by bright red Dutch barns, each topped by a white belfry-like construction. There were woods, hillsides, valleys and streams. It would have looked better without the gloom, it's true, but, like some pretty girls, it didn't need to put on its most fancy dress to look good.

It continued like that next day, too, and in weak sun and without the expansion joints. It was our most beautiful day since the Adirondacks. We climbed more than we descended, through crops-and-cows country—Ayrshires for the novelty, Holsteins for ubiquity—past a farm every half a mile. This was once more agriculture to human scale, every farm with its little white house, and beside each house a cylindrical steel silo like a fat cigar tube.

The road surface made friends with us and the scenery set out to woo. On a plateau the crops ended and grass the shade of Irish green took over. The fields probably grew things, although it was hard to say what. They looked as though they had been sown with grass for our pleasure, although now and then we passed a field of sticks and stalks of old crops harvested and then removed. Some had been overlaid with regular lines of new growth.

Long-stemmed grass blew in the wind, like shaking sheets. All day we were sung to by blackbirds, not even soot like their European cousins but black with red shoulders. And every few minutes a fussy brown bird with a white or cream undercoat and a dark lower trailing edge to its wings would totter ahead of us on spindly legs, like a child trying her mother's high heels. It was a diversion, a parent offering itself as bait to distract us from young nesting somewhere unseen. Some had perfected moving with a limp or a trailing wing to appear easy prey. But move close and off they would go in perfect health, wheeling through the air, their job done, not returning to the nest until we were too far away to notice.

There were no flying geese, though. Other times we watched as they flew in a V towards us and then, close to shooting range, turned off in a half-circle to keep at a safe distance. I never realized geese were that clever until the BBC sent me to the North Sea coast on a gray winter's morning in eastern England. A game warden pointed it out; Darwinian selection had taught geese to see danger in humans in exposed places and taught them the range of their shotguns.

Léo Woodland

We rejoined the Mississippi in Marquette, riding beside or within sight of it to Red Wing. Steamboats trailed the water here in the 19th century. Passengers boarded and disembarked at small towns like Lansing and farmers brought grain to its mills. A man called James Metcalf wrote:

> What a tremendous business was that of the steamboat lines, in those times, in carrying pleasure-seekers from the south to Minnesota points! What fine steamers loaded to capacity, were those of the Diamond Jo and the Packet Companies, rivals in trade! And the river traffic in lumber was marvelous. I have sat upon my porch, at my home fronting the river, Sunday afternoon for example, and there was scarcely a moment when the river, fronting and above and below Lansing for a short distance, was free from rafts, passing down stream, and always interesting to observe, aside from the fact of the immense interests in business which they represented.

> Socially there were no finer, more generous folk than those of the old time in Lansing. My life has not been uneventful, and I have mingled with people in every part of the country, but I have yet to know of a place where the residents were more social, more hospitable, more friendly to a stranger, than those of the town nestled at the foot of Mount Hosmer.

But things weren't always so smiling. I picked up the *Courier Press* and looked through stories of how life used to be around here. One told us:

"Steamboat explosions were an unfortunate risk for travelers in the middle of the 1800s. The accident didn't have to happen; the young pilot, Captain Perkins, pushed the engine to save time when he made stops. He didn't release the steam valve but kept a full head up. People thought he was foolish for taking such a risk, but he always filled his boat because he made such good time. The boat was about 30 feet from shore when it just blew apart and sank within 15 minutes. Almost all the two hundred passengers were killed. Captain Perkins was discovered in the street, his body mangled. He had been launched more than 50 feet by the explosion."

We passed through a countryside of conical or bread-shaped hills like molds of green jelly. Their densely wooded sides hid the underlying orange soil. From the sky it looked like sponge countryside made for a model railway. We rode through rising valleys of pastures and woods; we passed in awe of bluffs that towered above us and recalled the Lot and Céré valleys in southern France. We rode beside the Mississippi, broad and dappled with enough mud islands to keep Tom Sawyer happy until the last page. Broad, shallow ponds greeted birds and beasts between the road and the river, a nature park where white lilies paved the water's surface but refused to show their petals, too scared of the cold day. We were happy.

At Pickwick we rattled down a hill of potholes and ridges and stopped with arms aching and eyebrows revolving where a bridge fenced in wood crossed the end of the beautifully named Big Trout Creek.

"They've been planning to mend that road for 10 years," said the taller of two bikies who stopped to chat. We were sitting at a table beside the appealing wooden water mill. "Can you see them ever getting round to it?" All four of us laughed at the expense of road menders and their promises everywhere.

Pickwick is named after Charles Dickens and the novel he wrote. The mill was about all there was in the years after the first settlers arrived in 1854. One of them, George Grant, built it and brought grinding stones from France. They turned day and night to supply Union troops during the Civil War. The area needed a name, though. For want of anything better, locals accepted the suggestion of a woman called Mary Davis who had enjoyed *Pickwick Papers*. And so the village became Pickwick.

I like old industrial buildings with their big wooden wheels and leather belts and the way, like a bicycle, you can understand what everything is supposed to do. Pickwick's charm is that it stands, or rather balances, through the design of its structure. Not a single metal nut or bolt holds it in place. Wooden wedges close gaps and keep things where they are but, otherwise, all six stories stand where they are through the skill of their designers and carpenters.

The mill ground flour and livestock meal for 120 years until the sluices closed and the wheel fell still in 1978. Two years later the building was torn apart by a rare flood. It took the people of Pickwick two years to form a rescue association and start bringing the mill back to life.

Léo Woodland

Outside, as we left, half a dozen lads gathered on the bridge. They wore baggy shorts to their knees and nothing else. They were picking up courage to throw themselves off the bridge and a debate was going on about who was going first. Two of the boys, and only two, were slim. The others, at 10 or 11, had flab overflowing the waist of their shorts. Their backs were lined where gravity pushed one layer of fat down over the one below it. Double chins were standard. I read that the percentage of American children riding bikes or walking to school dropped from 41 percent in 1969 to 13 percent in 2001; obesity among children rose from 6.5 percent in 1980 to 19.6 percent in 2008.

I'm not the first to point out that Americans are fat. Not just some but most. They are, politely put, overweight or they are fat or they are shockingly obese. Even Americans who doubtless considered themselves of "normal" weight looked as though they'd had a few more breakfasts than they'd seen mornings. And it's not only the obese who have trouble walking. Going anywhere but by car is so strange to many Americans that, even if they are not excessively fat, they seem to have lost the ability to walk. They look as though their brains are struggling to remember what they learned as infants but have rarely practiced since. When sociologists say obesity is the prime problem facing America, it is easy to agree.

There are many things to see in a journey of months but, equally, there are some that time forbids. We declined, for instance, the chance to see the world's largest boot, in Red Wing. There were signs to it and I can't say that we weren't tempted, for it's not every day you see a boot 16 feet high and 20 feet long. But it was cold and the rain was falling in rods and it seemed more attractive to find coffee and Sticky Buns.

We did ask about it, though. It turned out that the Red Wing Shoe Company celebrated its centenary in 2005. And what better way to mark it than create a giant boot? The cobblers took it round the country, showing it off at county fairs and so on, and people gasped and took pictures and told friends of what they had seen. It stands now in a museum in Main Street. It is, incidentally, a left boot. Or it looks that way from photos, anyway.

We passed more riders coming the other way, some crossing the country in one go, others in installments.

"Tell us about Sam," we asked.

"Oh yes," they said. "We met him a couple of days back."

"Which means he must be two or three days ahead of us."

"Must be by now. He'd like it if you caught him. He said he's feeling lonely."

"Where did he say he came from?"

"Said he was from France but he sounds British."

We crossed from Wisconsin into Minnesota, then back again as mood, roads and bridges took our fancy. States do things differently. And traffic clings to one bank of a river more than the other. Along the west bank of the Mississippi is Route 61. Its number was in a shield, which means a busy road. It's hard to avoid because there is little choice across the valley, but it's busy, noisy, it smells of engine fumes and its broad shoulder—in America drivers expect you not to use the road you have paid for—is cracked and has an expansion joint every few turns of the pedals. Across on the other side the road had a circled number: quieter, better for cycling. It followed the river in just the same way and we couldn't be worse off unless it was all but plowed. We couldn't lose.

We rode over the bridge in Winona and set off down the other bank. We couldn't have been happier. The road was quiet and the bike path generous and silky smooth. There were sweet views of the river. Even the coal-fired power station was creamy clean. The road ran beside the green bluffs of the Wisconsin ridge without challenging them. At one point the railroad passed beneath the bluffs. Close to Cochrane, train drivers have found, is the perfect stretch to sound the locomotive's horn. American trains have a long, mournful, soulful horn. And every time one reaches Cochrane, the driver opens his window, gives a good long hoot and enjoys the echo that falls back off the bluff.

"Did you know train engineers have their own distinctive way of blowing the horn?" an old guy in a bar asked us when we heard yet another hoot and yet another echo. He was about 70, dressed in blue jeans, pointed-toe boots, a red polyester windcheater and a baseball cap. Pretty much uniform for 70-year-olds along the Mississippi. "Don't know for sure that's still the case but it used to be that way when I was a boy round here. Got that we knew one engineer from another, even if we never knew their names."

"Much else to do round here?" we asked.

Léo Woodland

He looked at us, amused.

"Nope."

He must have been missing out. There were two bars in town. Across the road and up a side street was the 5th Avenue bar—"Drinks, Food, Fun." The black and white illuminated sign showed a rabbit sitting in grass. Pretty gentle fun, then, probably. But, wait... Beneath the sign, just a little higher than the neon Budweiser sign, the one there is in every bar window in America, hung a scarlet sign with white capitals. "Deer and Turkey Registration Center," it said. Now, *that's* living. In Wisconsin it is, anyway.

In fact, they have an odd sense of fun here. Just back from Cochrane—pronounced Cock Rain, seemingly without embarrassment—was the Prairie Moon sculpture garden and museum. There was little warning of it and so suddenly there you are beside a wall of alternating red arches and cones, the first topped by a coconut-like affair decorated by stones, the second by a golden wizard's cone. The arch stands on white and red bricks built into round pillars. The whole lot reaches 260 feet along the road and delightfully serves no purpose at all. It could keep nothing in nor nothing out.

"You could go around the world five times and never see another like it," said the garden's three-page folder with striking accuracy. The story is that Herman Rusch, the son of a couple who'd immigrated from East Prussia, made a name as a fiddle player, worked as a farm hand and then retired in 1952. Time hung on his hands and he started to collect anything that nobody else was likely to collect. Like, for instance, a washing machine powered by a goat walking inside a treadmill. Not many people collect those. He filled a hall and turned his attention to the grass outside. And that he filled with dinosaurs, a Hindu temple, animals eating each other, some windmills and a long snake. With a few that he bought from a sculptor every bit as daft as he was, he ended up with close on 40 sculptures by the time he died in 1985.

The collection was dispersed. The new owners of Prairie Moon, metaphorically reaching for their gun at the mention of "art", used the pavilion as a dog kennel. That upset Rusch's fans and by 1994 they'd gotten things back in order. They gave it to the local council as public art and there it stands, behind a red wall the like of which you could travel the world five times without seeing copied. A triumph of eccentricity.

Sticky Buns Across America

Back when we were in New York, we spent the night in Medina. It's a pleasant town, old by American standards, that has resisted tearing down its heavy, square turn-of-the-century buildings. The result was gravitas instead of the flimsy feel that American towns so often give. On the edge of town was a railroad museum run by a fair-haired man, a retired fireman and now an amateur drummer, called Marty Phelps. Outside stood a huge, gray diesel locomotive from the New York Central. Across the tracks was the old freight house, which Marty has filled with scale locomotives in cases, a model railway that takes several minutes to walk round, and a collection of helmets from his fire-fighting past.

"I started the collection years back," he told us. He fussed about us as though he had spent the whole day waiting for us to arrive. He was one of those people you knew instantly that you liked. He's 66 and I don't doubt that, like most men, he started running model trains when he was a kid but, like most men, doesn't regret at 66 that he ever stopped. Because he never did. "People have added their own collections since then and we've incorporated those as well. And we're still building. We moved here seven years ago and now it's all protected by state law and no one can touch it."

It took him all the length of catching his breath before he offered us a *caaahfee*. And then another breath to ask where we planned to sleep. We said we were thinking of going on closer to Niagara Falls.

"Stay here if you like," he said. "Look…" He took us outside and pointed to yellow marquees erected along the side of the museum for a Thomas the Tank Engine weekend. "Pitch your tent inside. Why not? Gonna be a storm tonight and your tent'll stay dry in there. We've had other folks stay. Make yourself at home. I'll leave the rest rooms open for you and I'll tell security you're here, so they'll keep an eye on you." And so we slept with our tent inside another tent.

Now, I tell you this because it was yet another example of spontaneous American generosity. But the main reason is that on the wall of the rail museum, along with all the helmets, a giant green bean advertising soup, a chart explaining when and where to oil a steam locomotive and advertisements for long-vanished expresses, was a red wooden sign about the length of your forearm and a little taller than your hand. On it was written "Burma-Shave."

Burma-Shave is one of those bits of Americana for which I have false nostalgia. Entirely false because I never saw the signs the company put up, still less remember them. Burma-Shave was made in Minneapolis, near where we were now. Radio stations playing in Sticky Bun joints and gas stations are from what we have learned to call the Twin Cities: Minneapolis and its older neighbor, St. Paul. In the western suburbs of Minneapolis is an area known as Bryn Mawr, and there early in the 20th century two brothers called O'Dell started the Burma-Shave company. They made liniment but nobody wanted it. Not to rub on their limbs, anyway. But change the formula and perhaps they'd put it on their chin. And so they made Burma-Shave shaving cream.

Their problem was that they had no money, the liniment not having sold and the shaving cream having been expensive to make. So in 1925 they hit on spending Monday, Tuesday and Wednesday on the road, staking advertisements on the verge. They ran in batches, 100 feet apart, red with white letters, each with one line of a rhyme. "Drove too long… driver snoozing… what happened next… is not amusing… Use Burma-Shave." On Thursday and Friday they stopped at shops and garages to ask how many orders they'd had.

Storekeepers were relieved to find what it was all their customers were talking about. It was easy to sell them a crate or two. By the end of the 1950s the O'Dell brothers were earning $900,000 a year. A fortune. And then they sold their company to Philip Morris, the tobacco company. The barons missed the point that the roadside ads were the heart of the business. People the right side of 50 remember them with fondness even now. Where the brothers hadn't always troubled to pay for the land on which their signs stood, Philip Morris spent $150,000 a time, as much in 60 seconds on television during football game as the brothers had earned in 60 days. By the end of the season the game was over. And then the signs went, victim of faster travel and, ironically, of concerns for road safety which they themselves had promoted. They were tokens of when travel was slow enough to enjoy. Like riding a bike. Fast enough to get somewhere, slow enough to amuse.

No Burma-Shave and no Minneapolis for us, though. Instead, a rolling ride to the busy and bumpy town of Stillwater, a mayhem of traffic, antiques shops and antiquarian book stores. It stood not on the Mississippi but the St. Croix. The name means "Holy Cross" in French. It probably does in America, too, but here it's pronounced *San Croy*." We took the bridge across the San Croy and we were away from the traffic again.

Minnesota is an appealing state. It's the 12th largest, we found, but an awful lot is under water. "The land of 10,000 lakes," they call it. In fact—and for heaven's sake, someone has counted them—there are 11,842. They lie beside the road, across on the other side of fields and behind crops of trees. Some are large and some are ponds. I don't know whether they counted the ponds as well. Nor the frogs. Frogs barked at us wherever we went. I picked up a tourist brochure for Mille Lacs Lake,

Minnesota: we entered a universe of calm and of wheat

which means "One Thousand Lakes Lake" and, here if not by the French explorers who named it, is pronounced *Milly Lacks*. "Because of recent droughts," it said, "the water level is down in Lake Mille Lacs. So someone asked the question: 'How much water would it take to raise Lake Mille Lacs one foot?'

"With a surface area of 207 square miles, the answering is a staggering 43,168,797,257 gallons. (That's 43 BILLION, one hundred sixty-eight MILLION...!) Here's another way to picture that amount of water. If you filled 12-ounce pop cans with water and stacked them end to end, they would reach to the moon *and back* 36 times!" They adore capitals, italics and exclamation marks in these parts.

Léo Woodland

Something else that distinguished Minnesota was its fight to save Main Streets, the town centers that grew up over a century as the town expanded around them. They developed a personality, an appearance, a charm. People walked and talked and gossiped. They *were* the town. Now the streets are still there but the shops have gone. There is little reason to go there any more. Traffic increases, a town prospers but the automobile is displeased. It takes too long to get anywhere with towns every ten miles. The remedy for decades: build a bypass. Traders followed the traffic. They moved to the edges, a soulless district chosen only because there was space. You have to drive there and you drive from one store to the next. Unless you ride a bike, of course, and nobody but a crank rides a bike.

A vortex happens when Walmart arrives. The stores are so vast and the prices so low that they suck life out of all who dare to compete and then the breath from town centers because, for their very size and the airport-like parking lot, they can't be built where people live. Towns fight to keep Walmart out. But people shop there. And, deprived of anywhere more local and forced to drive their cars, they go some distance to do so. Time and again, when traffic was busy as we left a town, we guessed there was a Walmart ahead. As soon as we passed it, two thirds of the traffic vanished.

To quote Josie Dew again, talking of her mother's town: "[It] is a fine example of small-town America wrecked by out-of-town monster mega-malls. A small downtown store which had once been run by one of my far-off relations was now boarded up and derelict, as were the majority of those interesting, topsy-turvy buildings lining Main Street that must once have given the town such character. Instead of walking downtown to 'real quaint' family-run stores, everybody now drove a few miles down the road to shop in an enclosed expanse of sprawling, character-less concrete."

Minnesota is trying to reverse the trend. We saw signs advertising towns as Main Street communities, places that had kept their soul.

"Many of us long for a time when our Main Street was the thriving commercial and social hub of our community," says the state's Preservation Alliance. "Established residents talk of going to town for everything they needed, from a can of soup to a car, gasoline to gossip, and all things in-between." I got in touch with Emily Northey at the alliance. It'd be sad, I said, to think there was no more than signs and goodwill. But, no, no, she gasped. Take Brainerd, for instance. Nineteen businesses had moved into the area or expanded there in the last year. Together they'd taken on 27 more people. And then Faribault, she said breathlessly... Five new businesses there, one, always a hub of a community, a barber shop.

"The *Minneapolis Star* said the town was brimming with new life, charms worth discovering," Emily said. "And downtown Red Wing's already known for well-preserved historic buildings, but the improvements continued this year with over $880,000 of facade renovations completed. They've installed 20 new bike racks, 20 new bike trail signs, and put new pavement down along the Riverfront Bike Route. They're now working on improving pedestrian crosswalks downtown and across Highway 61." And don't even get me started on Willmar and the farmers' market that's been so successful there that it looks like becoming a year-round store, she seemed to say...

There was a Main Street in Lake Wobegon, the village that never appears on maps because surveyors in Minnesota started both from the east and the west. Their calculations were several miles out when they met in the middle. Rather than start again, they stitched together what they had mapped and ignored the gap. That is where, Garrison Keillor insisted, Lake Wobegon lay.

Lake Wobegon, said Keillor in his slow drawl, is "a quiet town, where much of the day you could stand in the middle of Main Street and not be in anyone's way—not for ever, but for as long as a person would want to stand in the middle of a street. It's a wide street; the early Yankee promoters thought they would need it wide to handle the crush of traffic. The double white stripe is for show, as are the two parking meters."

In Lake Wobegon, Mr. Tollefson climbs to the top of the Norge Co-op grain elevator, the highest point for miles, and flies the flag on national holidays and the Norwegian flag on Norwegian Independence Day. Almost every Norwegian who emigrated to the New World between 1815 and 1860 settled in Wisconsin, Minnesota, Iowa and Illinois. Heaven knows why because I can't think of a place that less resembles fjords and mountains.

Keillor wrote of conflicts between Lutheran settlers from Norway and Catholics from Germany "who, bound for Clay County, had stopped a little short, having misread their map but refused to admit it." Lake Wobegon may be fictional but the radio series that spawned it, the Prairie Home Companion, began in Minnesota in the very real town of St. Paul. Keillor told of stolid and bickering residents burdened by war between what the humorist Frank Muir summed up as "the strict, low church of the Protestants—the young author and his family belonged to a particularly bleak sect called the Brethren—and the much jollier and more colorful religion of the Catholics."

The division went deep.

"In Lake Wobegon," Keillor intoned, "car ownership is a matter of faith. Lutherans drive Fords, bought from Bunsen Motors, the Lutheran car dealer, and Catholics drive Chevys from Main Garage, owned by the Kreugers. Pastor Tommerdahl knew for a fact that the Kreugers spent a share of their Chevy profits to purchase Asian babies and make them Catholics."

To unite this argumentative community, someone decided to create a Living Flag. Everybody would be given a red, white or blue cap and be organized so that, from above, they would look like the Stars and Stripes. The trouble was that those who were under rather than over the caps could see nothing of what they had created. When someone suggested an overhead mirror, everyone looked up and saw nothing but their faces looking back down. So they took it in turn to run up the stairs of a neighboring building, look down and hurry back to let the next man run up. All this, naturally, took time and even the most stolid Lutherans grew cross. The day was not a success.

Well, you may think life never gets that good. Except that the story is true. The idea, anyway. In 1917 thousands of American soldiers lined up on a sports field to form the Liberty Bell. And that done—as photographs show—other crowds created the American flag, the Statue of Liberty and even the face of the president, Warren G. Harding.

To ride through Minnesota even now is like living out Garrison Keillor. Norwegian flags hung from houses. There were Lutheran churches. And then in the local paper, two items. The first: "Sons of Norway Lodge 1-364 will meet at…. Laurann Gilbertson, Vesterheim Norwegian-American Museum's textile curator, will present an armchair tour of Vesterheim's newest exhibit: 'Pieces of Self-Identity and Norwegian-American Quilts.' Several local quilts made by Big Canoe Ladies Aid, Highland Ladies Aid and Lena Werson will be included in her presentation. People attending are invited to bring quilt stories to share."

And then, more touching, the obituary of a girl of three killed in a car crash. It said: "She had pride in knowing all her letters and sounds and could write her family's names and count to 10 in Norwegian." Across the river in Minnesota, the *Dorset Daily Bugle* (motto: "Published once a year whether there's news or not!") reported on page three—there are only four pages—

'Lutefisk Wednesdays' added to menus

Scandinavians who just can't get enough of their lutefisk will no longer have to wait for those church basement Christmas dinners to enjoy the codfish delicacy now that Dorset's restaurants are featuring lutefisk-inspired dishes to their menus on Wednesdays. Culinary specialties using the mouth-watering delicacy include:

- Lutefisk skillet breakfast featuring free-range lutefisk mixed with potato dumplings and creamed peas, all browned in lard, with pickled pigs feet on the side.

- Lutefisk burritos, with boiled (is there any other way?) cod and cream-style corn wrapped in lefse and topped with mild mustard, as well as a cup of melted butter for dippers.

- Lutefisk and roasted turkey combo with rutabaga chips, lime Jell-O with shredded carrots and, for dessert, Grandma's fruitcake.

- Lutefisk and herring pizza with ketchup sauce and sprinkled with grated Velveeta, all on a plain white crust, with a glass of Kool-Aid.

In an agreement with Park Rapids residents, Lutefisk Wednesdays will be canceled when the wind is blowing to the west.

I have a friend in New England who, although he is white, checks the box for African-American when confronted by a census form. He does this not from bloody-mindedness, although he is not unaware of the small blow he is making against nosiness. He does it because he is indeed an African American. He was born in what used to be Rhodesia and is now Zimbabwe. He moved to England and became British, then moved to America and became American. He is an African American as well as an American African. Among many cultural changes he noticed on crossing the Atlantic was, as the British author Julian Barnes put it, that a foreigner in the USA can make his country disappear simply by picking up a newspaper. There is barely any reporting from outside the USA, in print, on radio or on television. His local radio station, my friend boasted, boasted "All the world's news, coast to coast."

American television isn't much cop if you want to know what's happening further west than California or to the right of Maine. But it is indispensable if you have piles, rheumatism or knocking knees. Even, in fact, if you have none of these but long to be ill with something. On occasional nights we holed up in motels. Usually it was because it was raining or had been raining and we wanted to dry out. Once or twice it was because it was too hot. It was 35C degrees or more many days, wilting weather, weather when the physiological need to drink is outweighed by the warm syrup of water that has spent the past hour heating up in a plastic bottle.

In Aitkin, where Judy Garland once performed in a store and the cinema is a charming remnant of those days, we holed up because of a tornado. "Tornado" is a Spanish word but I'm not sure tornados exist in Europe. Not in the way they are a feature of the USA, where weather men speak of "tornado seasons" as though they were tomatoes. That night we listened to the rain, watched to see if the hotel sign would blow away, lost interest when it didn't and turned on the television. It began beeping, and beeping loudly. We didn't know it was the television and we began looking round the room. Was it on fire? Had a burglar broken in?

It turned out to be, as any American would know but most Europeans wouldn't, a tornado alert. Across the bottom of the screen ran text telling us that tornado alerts had been issued for a whole string of counties, none of which meant anything to us. We went back to the window and looked beyond the gas station across the road to see what an approaching tornado might look like. Was a tornado the same as a whirlwind? Could we expect to be lifted to the Land of Oz?

In fact it was disappointing. The wind blew, rain poured but drivers kept going up and down and the gas pumps weren't sucked into the sky. We went back to watching television. It was showing an ad for something that "more than four million Americans may suffer without knowing it." Isn't that the perfect sales line? You don't know you have this illness but you ought to buy medicine anyway. After all, it's not just you: 3,999,999 other Americans don't know they've got it either. In which case you wonder how they could be counted.

Bill Bryson, the American writer who spent two decades in Britain before moving home, wrote: "I monitored the NBC evening news last night. This is one of the main national news programs, the equivalent of the BBC's *Six o'Clock News*, but with the addition of several minutes of advertising for dental fixtures, hemorrhoid creams and laxatives. (People who watch the evening news in America are evidently in a bad way.) Later, I undertook a similar exercise with CNN's main evening bulletin. It lasted an hour, so it offered even more adverts for painkillers, salves and mentholated unguents (somebody really should get these viewers to hospital) but also managed to squeeze in 22 snippets of news, of which all 22 were about the United States. This on a program that calls itself *The World Today.*"

I'll say this for local radio in America, though—it is so desperate for international content—any content—that it interviewed us. The background is that some years ago I saw a T-shirt with the legend "Hike faster: I hear banjo music." It was in the Appalachians, the mountains of the eastern USA that Europeans have never heard of and where hikers spend endless days in the woods and give themselves names like Bed Bug and Snot Guy. It was quite a surprise when a sweet, bespectacled lady in a library looked up from her list of candidates for the internet and called: "Flatulence Boy, it's your turn."

Well, it was banjo music we heard in the single town between Aitkin and Grand Rapids. It's called Hill City because the road rises a dizzying 10 meters before settling down to its former quiet existence. We were being blown at lightning speed by the wind that persisted after the tornado. The banjo was part of a three-man jazz band, dressed in flowery blue shirts, playing outside a bank on the edge of town. The musicians waved us over. A small crowd was around them and a table drawn up behind and the place had the air of a party.

"Best jazz trio for miles around," an admirer said. "From the Twin Cities." That gave us a sense of achievement: we knew where the Twin Cities were. The musicians, two gray panthers with glasses and embryonic bellies and a dark-haired youngster in his 40s who played trombone in that uncontrolled way that trombonists have, as though only shaking the thing will produce a sound, asked about our trip. They showed a lot of enthusiasm, shook our hands, then took their time from the banjo player on the left and began another tune. It was then that someone took Steph by the elbow and said: "We'd love to have you on the radio."

To one side was a black van with windows, on its door the word "KOZY", a radio station in Grand Rapids. Beside the front wall of the bank was a short, distracted woman with a microphone, headphones and a cup of coffee on a thong. Grand Rapids, she said, was too far to use the radio car and she was having to broadcast four interviews an hour for four hours at phone quality. Which, I can tell you as a former BBC broadcaster, is a shameful position technically that could only suggest the bank had paid a lot for the station to cover the opening of a new branch.

Our radio connections—Steph was an electronics engineer with the BBC and, to her dismay, turned up as a blue-eyed blonde in recruitment brochures—were an instant "in". But nobody could have guessed that we shared our name with the Woodland Bank. It was fun and we chatted and then set off back up the hill. Just how transient is fame became clear when we stopped for eggs on toast. We told the waitress what had happened. She had the station playing in the cafe.

"Can't say I listen to it, though," she said. "Not much chance if I got meals to serve…"

4

Leos are born between July 23 and August 22, fitted queen-size sheets measure 60 by 80 inches, and America is the greatest country on earth

We'd met Donn Olson just back along the road. Another Scandinavian name and with two Ns in his first because his mother hoped he would never be called Donald. Mothers have odd ideas. It's Donalds who are called Don, not Dons who are called Donald.

Anyway, Donn one day felt sorry for passing cyclists and built them a bunkhouse with three bedrooms, toilet, shower, tables, chairs, a microwave and a coffee machine. He provided cutlery and cups and apologized that he hadn't gotten round to providing pizzas. And he wasn't joking. It all stands just inside the entrance to his farm outside Dalbo, a village of 80 in gentle, watery countryside among townships called Lindstrom and Malmo.

There is a combined bar and restaurant in Dalbo. We stopped, doused ourselves in sticky drinks and a beer, and waited for something to happen. I don't know what. There are times, when you're tired and in the cool, you seek reasons to stay a little longer. We had just given up hope when something did happen. Paul arrived in gray shorts and a yellow T-shirt. He had a little gray beard and a mustache, he was sweating gently, he looked flustered and he was seriously in need of a beer.

"They say there's a cyclists' hostel near here," he said in a light accent that betrayed his origins in Germany. He moved first to Canada and then to the USA, where he lives just south of Seattle. He has lived in America for 50 years. His longest bike tour was from the north to the south of Africa, from Cairo to Cape Town. Today, he was riding another stage of a trip from Vancouver to eastern Canada. "You know where the hostel is? I came in here to ask."

"No you didn't," we teased. "You came in here for a beer and *then* you were going to ask."

He smiled and we sent for more beers. Only then did we ride the mile or two out of the village towards Ogilvie (quite the metropolis with 474 residents). On the right, on a slight slope, stood a flag pole with spotlights ready to be turned on, and a white wooden board painted with a bicycle and the words "Adventure Bicyclists Bunkhouse." A typed sign pinned to a post explained:

1. Make yourself at home. (No need to check in with us.)

2. It's OK to bring your bikes inside

right down to

8. See me for recommended changes to your planned bike route to take advantage of Minnesota's bike trails. Heading east or west, I can make it easier for you.

We walked inside. Everything was in wood, the walls of pale planks and the ceiling held up by beams supported by vertical posts. One of the beams had been branded BICYCLE BUNK HOUSE with a hot poker. Armchairs and a table filled the space. To one side was a makeshift kitchen with a refrigerator, coffee-maker, kettle microwave and a pizza oven. There was coffee and sugar. There were three bedrooms with mattresses on wooden frames. A notice board displayed maps, tourist leaflets, explanations of bike trails and grateful messages from those who had passed earlier. Outside was a lavatory and an elementary shower.

I looked through the guest book. Evgeny, a 26-year-old Russian, had been on the way to Seattle. Harry and Rita Rottiers turned out to be the two Belgians just ahead of us. And there, too, was a message from Don, the man in desert boots who had fallen out with his riding companion back in Monroeville. Nothing from Sam, though.

Donn arrived, a tall, strong, square-headed, fair-haired man of 62, just the sort to have a name like Olson. His hair was short and he wore glasses, blue jeans and a checkered shirt. To shake hands was to be enveloped and close to crushed by a man who spent much of his life hauling timber and shifting machinery. He said he would all but kidnap passing cyclists to get them to spend the night.

"You know how it started?" he asked. "They re-laid the road outside a while back and these guys came by, pushing their bikes because of the gravel. They were all in and they came up to the house and knocked on the door and asked if there was anywhere on the farm they could camp. They just couldn't go any further. Well, they told me all about bike touring—I mean, I ride a bike, but just a mile and a half down to the shops, not like you guys—and they told me about the Adventure Cycling Association and I was impressed with what they were doing."

Donn retired from farming and looked for things to do. He had a cow byre that had stood unused since his parents got out of dairy farming because arable paid better. He'd make a bunkhouse for cyclists.

"I still keep my hay up in the loft—I sell it to horse riders and there's no one more particular than someone with ponies—but the ground floor was free, so I put in beams to keep the whole lot from collapsing, and the whole lot just balances, one timber on another, without a nail to hold it." The beams came from a single oak on his ground. Donn knows about trees. "I'm a tree guy," he said. He has rented his workable land to another farmer and he's turned the rest into a cross between a park and a nature reserve. He took the three of us on a tour of the estate. We bumped through small woods maintained for the pleasure of being among trees and then we stopped.

"See those two deer across there?" Donn asked.

We looked. Two deer were grazing but not moving.

"Concrete, they are. Someone down in the village had them and didn't want them outside the house any more. I said I'd have them and we put them on the back of a truck and brought them up here. Well, when my wife saw them she said she wasn't going to have them outside our house either. So I brought them up here and put them among the trees."

We smiled—America isn't strange to plastic and concrete animals outside its houses—but the story hadn't ended.

"Well, some while back, we had a bear around here. It didn't cause us any problems. Just used to nose about and then disappear. Then one day I came up here and one of the deer was lying on its side. Don't know just what happened, of course, but it certainly didn't just blow over in the wind. It's solid concrete, on a concrete base, and it weighs a ton. So I reckon the bear saw these deer and it licked its lips and it saw they weren't moving and he went for one of them. Must've had quite a surprise when he hit it."

Donn's family came from Sweden and bought land from the railway company, which wanted settlers, farmers and therefore freight business along its route. Germans established a community across the road and everyone began homesteading. I can't speak for the Germans but at least one church in the Dalbo area still holds services in Swedish.

"I can't speak Swedish," Donn said in Swedish, "but some of the old guys can and they love to get down to the church."

His parents had horses on the land. They fed them apples and the horses crapped the pips and the seeds took life readily in the manure with which they'd been delivered.

Donn sits, the only unelected member, on the town council and keeps saying he's happy to make room for someone elected except that nobody wants to dislodge him. And as if that weren't enough, he is head of deployment of military Chinook helicopters in the US. "I was in the military for decades, on Chinooks," he said. "Now I'm a contractor and I keep a record of where all the Chinooks are and I send them off to Boeing when they need to go. Course, they curse and grumble when I do it, because that leaves them short when I take them from somewhere that insists they need them. But I send them to Boeing and they strip out all the equipment and instruments and the airframes get scrapped. The Chinook is an old design, rivets everywhere. The new airframes are all in one place, not a rivet anywhere."

Posters of Chinooks decorate his office. There, too, framed, is a dollar. "The price of a house I sold," he explained. "There was this young couple and they didn't have much money and they asked if I'd sell an old house I had over the way. I said, well, yes, I could be interested in selling but they'd have to get the house off the land in a few weeks. If they could do that, they could have the house for a dollar. And so they made it happen and there you see the house being driven off down the road on a truck."

American houses are typically wood-framed and less substantial than European houses, which couldn't be winched or carted anywhere. But I do wish I'd asked how it was done, all in one piece.

There are several things in Grand Rapids. The first is Judy Garland's birthplace, a white wooden house that has been carried around town a few times until its final but possibly not permanent position across the road from a supermarket. The next is the waterfall, now dammed, that gives the place its name. And the second is a sticker on the back of a car that said "We're Number One because of our Veterans."

Veterans in America are old soldiers. Sailors and airmen, too, probably but it's soldiers who make a fuss about it. They grow old but refuse to fade away. They become Heroes—there seems no lesser status for soldiers even if all they served in was the pay corps—and they go on about it. It's not that the French hate their military, as that Hero's Wife insisted. It's just that, in France, being a soldier is seen as a job. Just a job.

But the point of this is not the insistence that old soldiers are to be thanked for America's fortunes but the assumption in the first place that America is "Number One." This tends to irritate people who aren't American. As the author David Sedars observed: "Every day we're told that we live in the greatest country on earth. And it's always stated as an undeniable fact: Leos are born between July 23 and August 22, fitted queen-size sheets measure 60 by 80 inches, and America is the greatest country on earth. Having grown up with this in our ears, it's startling to realize that other countries have nationalistic slogans of their own, none of which are "We're number two!"

Another sign, on a pickup, shouted: "Fuck you! I'm American. I'll drive wherever I want!" Not sure what that was about but the driver was angry about it.

Judy Garland's house, really, was just for fans. Worth a break to see what was there, followed by the feeling that there wasn't all that much but it had been interesting. She only lived there until she was four, anyway, and the fittings aren't original even if they're true to the era. The comical thing is that there is another exhibition across town in the museum, which even has a yellow brick road outside. The childhood house makes no mention of the museum; the museum mentions the childhood house but says nothing about its exhibition.

We camped beside the Mississippi on a site run by the engineering section of the army. When I asked why that should be, a round-faced, red-haired, belt-straining soldier told me the army looked after all the dams down the Mississippi. When I asked why that, too, should be so, he shrugged as if to say "It's always been that way" before adding "and it's a good deal better than being sent off to war." Catching what he had said and wondering if the PR people might object, he added importantly: "Course, we protect the dams against terrorists as well."

But not after 6pm, because that's when the soldiers go home.

We have yet to go through the main Indian reservations on our way to the Pacific but there are frequent reminders that this wasn't originally the White Fathers' land. There was a lot in the museum about the fate of the Ojibway. It didn't mention, as we found out elsewhere, that treaties between Indians and whites were so vague that they are still being fought in courts today. There was also trouble about the way Indians and whites saw land, the Indians believing it a resource held in common, the settlers as a commodity to buy and sell with whatever lay on it or below it.

Things didn't always go well and nor, the exhibits suggested, were treaties always honored in a way both sides expected. A panel explained:

> In 1837 the Ojibway agreed to the first in a series of sales by which the United States government acquired the forests and prairies that were to become Minnesota. The government's immediate interest in the then remote triangle of land between the Mississippi and St. Croix rivers was clearly stated by Governor Henry Dodge of Wisconsin Territory. 'Your Great Father wishes to purchase your country,' he told the Indians, 'for the advantage of its pine and timber, with which it is said to abound.' The Ojibway were willing to part with their land but not with their ancient way of life.

> 'In all the country we sell you,' said a chief known as The Trapper, 'we wish to hold on to that which gives us life—the streams and lakes where we fish, and the trees from which we make sugar.' Although the Government promised the Indians only the privilege of hunting, fishing and gathering wild rice on the ceded lands, 'during the pleasure of the President of the United States,' the Treaty of 1837 was quickly concluded, and the valuable pinelands of the St. Croix Delta became the property of the United States.

Sticky Buns Across America

Archdeacon Gilfillan recalled: "The Indians were very averse to making a treaty. They feared that in some way they would be in the end deceived and cheated, and it required a great many months of persuasion to induce them to sign. They realized that the pine was the last thing they had, and if they lost that all was gone. In order to make all as secure as they could they brought in a Bible and had the commissioners repeatedly swear both by kissing the book and with an uplifted hand, that that treaty would be honestly and fairly carried out. As one of the commissioners was a Roman Catholic bishop, they thought that his oath would be kept."

The American perception of history is, like that of most nations, often curious. Jesus, we found, was often portrayed as a white man. At best he had a sun tan. In a couple of cases he had blue eyes, which is less than usual in the Middle East. With his long hair he looked, as another writer put it, "like a Californian surfer dude."

The same goes with Indians. They were tall, noble, strong-boned and good looking. They stood sideways to the artist, the better to show off the hooked noses that every Indian had. And then you see a photo and you notice Indians were as ugly as anyone else. Effigy Mounds, on the edge of Iowa, was a wood of shallow domes of earth built in prehistoric times as religious monuments. European settlers expelled the Indians and plowed many of the mounds flat. They saw them as incomprehensible soil doodles of people too stupid to know why they were doing it. Since then there has been guilt over what America's settlers did there and more widely. But with how much overcompensation? Explanations at Effigy Mounds show Indians as peaceful, nature-loving folk who understood the movements of animals, the flow of rivers, and took no more from their surroundings than the surroundings could supply. They lived in harmony and peace.

Well, up to a point Lord Copper, as the obsequious newspaper editor says in *Scoop*. Indians didn't seek all the troubles they got from white men—several hundred died when the Ojibway resisted being thrown off their land—but they certainly fell out with each other. Tribes went to war, just as the white tribe went to war with them. The Ojibway were only in the area because they had driven out the Sioux and Fox in the first place.

The topic is too complicated for many Americans, let alone a European. But as outsiders, we wondered what part sentimentality and guilt played in the way that Indians are portrayed. And we looked forward to seeing, when we get to the reservations, how they are portrayed and treated now.

If Indians weren't welcome in the country invented around them, nor was Minnesota. North and South fell out over whether it should be a state rather than a vague territory, and whether foreigners there should vote on the strength of a promise to become American. Why give rights to "Norwegians who do not read one word of English?" asked the senator from Mississippi. "Who does not know that they are led up like cattle to the ballot-boxes, and vote as they are told to vote?" The man from Kansas said Minnesota should be run "as Great Britain rules Afghanistan, Hindustan and all the Punjab, making them work for you as you would work a Negro on a cotton or sugar plantation."

Yep, those were the days.

"You get bragging rights if you go to the source of the Mississippi," Donn Olson said as he fulfilled the promise to show us other routes. "You'd be better to go round this way though." And he ran his finger south and then west across the map, following a bike path created from an old railway line. "And it's hilly going up the Mississippi." But it's not every day you get to the source of a major river. We regret we didn't start at the source when we followed the Danube to the Black Sea. The Loire, France's longest river, doesn't start anywhere much. The Thames isn't worth bothering with. I remember a comedian called Michael Bentine set off to find its source, hacking through suburban washing lines with a machete. When he traced the first trickles with the pith-helmeted step of a Great Explorer, he found a dripping faucet. That's as exciting as the Thames gets.

The Ganges, the Danube, the Volga, the Mississippi… Those are *real* rivers. Having been at the mouth of the Mississippi in New Orleans, we weren't going to miss where it started. It was in New Orleans, by the way, that Steph was finally overcome by the persistent enthusiasm and friendliness of Americans. She covered her head in her hands and said: "Oh, stop being so fucking *cheerful!*"

We bowled on, northwards now, on a succession of days when everything was perfect. The sun shone, the pine-forest calm of countryside—the Leech Lake Indian reservation—was peaceful and unexploited, the roads quiet. For hour after hour we saw nobody and nobody saw us. There was the stretch, it's true, where three successive stretches had been left as soft sand and where Steph tumbled when her front wheel stuck in the first heap, but otherwise the skies smiled on us.

Then we met the group coming the other way. In front was an older man, behind him what may have been his two sons. We stopped to exchange tales and experiences. We were hit by a tsunami of arrogance. When we warned of roadworks where they planned to camp, the father knew all along. When it became obvious even to him that he couldn't know, he said he didn't intend to stop at that campground anyway.

"I prefer a place with showers and rest rooms," he said.

Who'd mentioned showers and rest rooms?

They had ridden from the Pacific, he said, talking but rarely listening. He asked how far we were riding and, with a touch of contempt at our efforts, told us they were "trying to do at least a hundred miles a day, although we got caught out by the weather coming across the Plains." The sons said nothing, perhaps because they never got the chance. Crossing America for them was an athletic challenge. I don't think they troubled to see the birth of the Mississippi. We felt sorry for them, but then they probably felt despairing of us.

At Becida, on the other hand, we were amused. Becida—pronounced *Beside-a*—is a crossroads. There is an improbably large restaurant with a single gas pump. The most exciting thing to happen there was when the little white, hall-like church, broke from its Lutheran origins. Those went back to 1898, when the pastor rode between his four churches on a horse. In 1970 the locals had enough of fjords and mountains and decided they weren't Lutherans any more. They became "a contemporary Spirit-filled congregation" boasting "We haven't walked this way before."

The restaurant was closed. We pressed our noses against the door and, Biblically, it opened. "We're not open for two hours but since you're here, come on in," said a tall man with a warm smile. He wore jeans, boots and a gray T-shirt with the name of the restaurant. He had a baseball cap of the sort that farmers wear. "There should be coffee if you want it."

We sat by the window. There was space for a visiting army. The polished brown wooden bar stretched into half darkness to our right. Some of the Budweiser signs were lit, others not. A vacuum cleaner stood silent, its lead snaking to a plug in the wall. The owner brought us coffee and went back behind the bar, talking to a man who could have been an old boxer or a Sicilian pizza cook. He wore the same gray T-shirt but his belly was bigger, his face heavier and his life gloomier.

"Storm today, they say," he was saying, enjoying anything about the world that was inconvenient. "As though we ain't seen enough of those."

"Keep the mosqueeters down, though," the owner said.

"Yeah, we ain't seen enough of mosquitoes yet, that's for sure. Gotta see a load more o' them before we're finished, that's for sure."

The man in the baseball cap shrugged. He turned on the TV above the bar. "There is a warning of flash floods in…," the dark-haired, over-primped woman was saying.

"We're gonna get some of them, that's for sure," said the former boxer or pizza chef.

"Not today, though," the other man said, determined to stop a spiral into suicide. "*Tomorrow*, they said, tomorrow."

"That on top o' everything else."

"Yep."

"World's gone crazy, that's for certain…"

The man in the cap stepped outside to wish us farewell. We said how much we'd enjoyed their exchange, one the optimist, the other determined to be grumpy. "Yeah, take no notice o' him. World-class grumbler. He's our cleaner but he likes nothing better than t'sit at the bar and moan a little. Stay safe, now, and watch out for those hills."

To be honest, we'd expected the Mississippi to be like Michael Bentine's faucet. There'd be a thin trail of water, then soggy grass and, beyond that, dry land. Between the wet and the dry would be where the Mississippi started. But it's not like that. The source of the Mississippi is wide enough that you need stepping stones to cross it. In fact it was moved to make it easier for visitors to do just that. It rises not from the ground but out of a lake. Given that water flows into the lake, you wonder why one of those other rivers isn't also the Mississippi and why the source of that isn't the source of America's longest, indeed even longer, river.

It seems it is so because a man with the leather-elbowed name of Henry Schoolcraft ruled it was so. The government sent him to sort out problems between the Ojibway and the Dakota. He took the chance to have a look at the Mississippi and got the Ojibway chief, Ozawindib, to take him up to Lake Itasca. It wasn't fun because he and the other 29—things weren't done by halves—had their patience tested by "voracious, long-billed and dyspeptic musketoes." They waded through mud, hauled their kit and reached what Ozawindib called Omushkos. Its other name was Lac la Biche, or deer lake, which makes you wonder if the French didn't get there first without knowing what they'd found. Maybe Schoolcraft thought he'd better declare this the source or he'd be wading through mud and musketoes for ever more. So, he got the credit, the Ojibway got 2,000 doses of smallpox vaccine, and the French got nothing.

In case anybody mistakes where he is, a pillar printed in gold capitals says: "Here 1,475 feet above the ocean the mighty Mississippi begins to flow on its winding way 2,552 miles to the Gulf of Mexico." Beside it, 16 flat stones offer a way to have your photo taken as you walk from one side to the other. Beside them, a three-year-old girl was crying because she had fallen into the water and wrenched her ankle. Her mother alternated between tending to her and giving her husband an "I told you you shouldn't let her do that" look.

Another mother was trying to explain life to a boy of about the same age.

"I want to go to the bathroom!"

"Honey, you can't, not here."

The boy had his finger on his fly, ready to let rip into the countryside. "Why not?"

"Because there are people about."

"But I do on the farm."

The mother looked round, embarrassed, and said: "We live on a farm." As though everybody hadn't been listening.

It seemed strange not to ride with the Mississippi any more. It had become part of our lives, at first broad at Muscatine, then narrower and shallower with every bridge. We shared it with Tom Sawyer and Huck Finn… "We catched fish and talked, and we took a swim now and then to keep off sleepiness. It was kind of solemn, drifting down the big, still river, laying on our backs looking up at the stars, and we didn't ever feel like talking loud, and it warn't often that we laughed—only a little kind of a low chuckle. We had mighty good weather as a general thing, and nothing ever happened to us at all—that night, nor the next, nor the next"…

Léo Woodland

And we shared it with Popeye and southern belles and the rear-wheel steamers of *Gone With The Wind*. It started in the middle of nowhere and flowed out through alligator country in a town as gaudy yet sensual as New Orleans. It had the romance to run north to south in a country that grew up east to west. It flowed as straight as any river might reasonably flow. It is the heart of America, its artery. Even I can see that, a European. And now we have left it, we began thinking that we were truly in Middle America. What Americans call flyover country because they see it from airplanes and are glad to fly over it. There were more woods, more rolling, but slowly the countryside became open, more arable, leaving the reeds and long grasses of drying wetland. We no longer heard the rising ratchet of frogs. Meadowlarks no longer limped to distract us from their young. We were moving closer to North Dakota, and North Dakota was the start of the long haul across the Plains of the north.

Almost the last village before we got there was Hitterdal. It is a crossroads with a rail freight line, broad, empty streets, a bank, a bed-and-breakfast, huge silos, a gas station and a drinks store. A small park stands beside the road with a pavilion provided by the Lions and a lavatory block and what looked like a polished gravestone that read "Hitterdal Centennial, June 29–July 1, 1984." We stopped in the park around noon because just down the road there'd been that dull thump of a snapping spoke. Steph's back wheel took on a wobble but still turned. If we spent the afternoon at the park, we could ride into Fargo next day—a Monday— and have my repair perfected at a bike shop.

We set up our little green tent beside some tables, nodded to a stocky man painting his house across the road. He was standing on a ladder, peering through a window, like a man conducting an elopement.

We settled down to replacing the spoke, wrenching off the cogs, pushing down hard in one direction with one hand while using the other to stop the freewheel spinning and undoing the good work. The man eloping gave us looks over his shoulder. He despaired of ineptitude he would never tolerate in his own workshop, and said: "Got tools and air if you need 'em. And coffee. Be glad to give you a tour of the premises, too." Because it wasn't his house after all.

It looked like one, with two windows on the ground floor and a door between them. The wooden fascia ran vertically at ground level and horizontally higher up, where another window sat square and centrally. The roof was flat. Just another building. Except that it turned out that Craig Mozeley and his wife Wanda, their daughter and her husband, ran one of two companies in the USA that renovates the micro-pumps that mix carbonated water and syrup in fizz machines. The back room has been extended into a workshop where pumps begin a new life for people like McDonalds.

Craig was 58. He plays bass in a bluegrass band with an immigrant from the Isle of Wight, just off southern England, who Craig said is in the Guinness Book of Records as the world's fastest banjo player. They get on well but, equally, they don't get much chance to fall out because the banjo star's English accent proves impenetrable and Craig has no idea what he's on about. But with talent like that…

"I thought I could play banjo until I heard this guy," Craig said. He and Wanda live a few miles out of the village, in a farmhouse by the lake. "I collect musical instruments," he said. "Wife says I got far too many of them." He shrugged nonchalantly in a way that suggested the instruments would stay for as long as he remained boss in the house.

Wanda's family is from North Dakota. She and Craig lived in California until they could stand the crowds, laws and the cost no longer. Twenty years ago a customer—Craig was a salesman then—offered to sell his pump-renovation business. It was the perfect deal between friends, much of the cost paid from profits over three years and with no interest. "He even taught me the job," Craig said in appreciation. "We did it all just on a handshake with no hassle." Then the desire to leave California became irresistible and Craig and Wanda moved to as close to North Dakota as available business space would permit. "In California they think up here they're still duking it out, with gunfights and cowboys on horseback," Wanda laughed with an ironic tone.

We were joined by an intelligent, inquiring man called Bobby, his life also sufficiently undemanding that we couldn't be resisted. We discussed history, Indians, the sexual habits of Amish people, the war and the state of the world. We talked about the weather—"The interesting thing about the weather here is that at any time of the year, it can kill you. People die of the heat in summer. In winter, and winter goes on a long time, it can get to minus 20. People break down or get stuck in snow drifts and they start walking for help and they die of the cold. You got to have a cell phone and survival gear"—and we were nowhere near through when Steph, troubled by so much wisdom, said she would buy something for our evening meal. The others looked astonished.

"But you don't understand," someone said. "We're holding a party for you tonight. We're going to cook a meal for you in the park. It's all arranged." That evening we ate outdoors, Craig and Wanda, Bobby and his wife Jess, Nick who is Craig and Wanda's lodger, Steph and me, a couple of adult passersby and several half-identified children who insisted their mothers knew where they were. It was a wonderful evening, one of those events that makes a ride, makes a life.

That evening, Bobby was troubled by Hitterdal's flag. It hung limp on its pole at the edge of the park. We'd seen thousands of flags and this looked no different.

"But it *is* different," Bobby said. "It's dirty. What d'you think? I should write a letter about it?"

He could see the pole from where he and Jess lived, with their daughter, Karma. Not at night, though, he couldn't, which raised a second point. The first was that the flag was dirty.

"Who'd I complain to about that?" he asked.

"The mayor, I guess," someone said.

"You think he's gonna do anything?"

"That's terrible, the way that is," Bobby said, emotional now. "I could take that down and wash it myself."

"Wouldn't do that."

"Why not?"

Nobody knew why not. Just that in everyday life you don't pull down public flags and wash them.

"Can't complain, can they, if they have their flag washed?"

Bobby's other point was that it should be lowered at dusk or it should be lit. Protocol demands the Stars and Stripes never hang in the dark. I forget how that was resolved. There didn't seem any chance of illuminating it and nobody seemed sure about taking it down at night and getting up at dawn to haul it up again. Least of all Bobby and Jess, who didn't feel they were natural early-risers. When we set off at nine next morning, there was no sign of movement when we went to their door to thank them. I pinned a note to their mail box instead.

I was so intrigued by this etiquette business that I looked it up. It turns out that nothing less than Chapter 1 of Title 4 of the United States

Code (4 USC § 1 *et seq*) covers it. It also turns out that while judges could fine people, the constitution says the judges would be acting illegally. So it is illegal to keep the flag up at night but it is illegal to punish anyone for doing so. It's no wonder there are so many lawyers in America.

The Plains started just after Fargo. The countryside was open before then but it was simply vacant afterwards. We rode for half a lifetime on a flat, straight, shelterless road. The wind blew against us. We watched a yellow plane spray crops and were sad when it stopped. An animal crossed the road far ahead and we spent a contented ten minutes discussing whether it was a cat. A man waved from a van. We took an unusual interest in barns. We passed a sign for Herefords but saw no cows. We saw nothing. There was an awful lot of that.

And then, down a side road which truck drivers' behavior suggested that nobody but they ever used, came the city of Ayr. Well, I say a city but it was a village. Although it wasn't even that. There was a straight dusty road that ran from the railroad, got as far as it could be bothered to go and then died out. It passed rows of gray, cylindrical grain silos so high that they cast afternoon shadow over much of North Dakota. And there was a combined café and post office that closed after lunch.

None of these attracted us there, although we'd have appreciated the café. We were there because an eccentric called Keith Johnson began collecting old buildings as a tribute to his son, Lonnie, who died in 1980. Don't look to me for an explanation: that's just the way it was. And the way it is now is that tucked back from the silos, and hidden in a swarm of mosquitoes, there is a turn-of-century town with no one in it. There was a Mobil gas station full of red pumps, clipboards for fan belts, tubs of oil and a uniformed and cap-wearing man pictured against red stripes as though he was planting the Stars and Stripes on a distant island. He held not a machine gun but an oil gun. "Mobilize for winter," he urged in fat italic capitals, greasing your differential being a patriotic act.

There was a complete flag in the one-room school house, along with three old bicycles, a mannequin schoolmarm in a long white dress and a model policeman. The policeman had impeccable teeth and his white-gloved hand emphasized the message on his chest: SLOW SCHOOL ZONE. I couldn't help remembering the message "Slow Children" painted on the road from time to time, wondering whether it warned drivers or assessed the mental faculties of local heirs and heiresses.

The store had its big roll of brown paper ready to wrap parcels, a big black stove with a long thin chimney, an advertisement for Orange Crush and white sacks, pinned to the wall, to offer Red Dog Wheat Flour. And so it went on, the barber shop with a striped towel over a chair to save the next customer from hair clippings, the ice cream parlor with its green lettering on the window and its soda fountains and big silver cash register, the rusty hanging triangle waiting to call firemen to the old fire engine. As another visitor observed, there are real towns in North Dakota with fewer habitable buildings than this.

Steph went off to find a local. She returned to say that an engineer working on the silos said Johnson was now in his 80s, that he lived away from the village and that he turned down offers to buy his ghost town. So there it stands, unsignposted, little visited, a pretty town with a good road and neat grass but no people.

There's a joke about North Dakota that says two farm hands were sent to Europe during the second world war. They had never been further than Fargo and they were overwhelmed by this ancient land of castles, cottages and legends.

"Hey," said one as he looked through a guide book, "we gotta go to Coventry. Says here that a naked woman rides through town on a horse."

His pal is impressed.

"Yeah," he enthuses. "We gotta go there. I ain't seen a horse for months."

The joke was one of Winston Churchill's favorites. I read there are so many horses in North Dakota—or conversely so few people—that there is a horse for every six inhabitants. North Dakota is the 19th largest state but 48th in population. North Dakota, South Dakota, Montana and Wyoming together are twice as large as France with a population less than south London. There are 256 people per square mile in France and more than 600 in Britain; there are slightly more than nine in North Dakota. There are only six in Montana.

A columnist called Dave Barry once joked about North Dakota's wish to make itself more exciting and stem its declining population by calling itself simply Dakota. The state responded by naming a sewage works after him in Grand Forks and inviting him to its opening—in

January. He said he unveiled his plaque to a cascade of plop, plop, plop—"the sound of people applauding in mittens."

What puts North Dakota in context is that it has an official soil. It has a state flower—the wild prairie rose—and an official bird (the western meadowlark) and an official drink (milk). *Milk* is the official drink of North Dakota? Well, after finding that tomato juice was the state drink of Ohio, I suppose milk is no odder. And I can just about see that if a state is going to pick a dance, it may as well be square dancing. You can do that in cowboy boots. But an official soil, for heaven's sake…

"Well, colleagues, we turn now from the state budget and the decline of our schools and the worrying future of industry and unemployment. There is our official soil to consider…" No sooner said than someone would pop up from somewhere called Hubcap or Drain City (pop. 35) and say: "The good and friendly people of Hubcap (or Drain City or Dogpiss Trickle) demand…" And someone would shout him down in the name of somewhere with a single gas pump and a lot of people with slightly crossed eyes and voices would rise and the evening would end in gunfire in the American Way. And all because nobody could agree on the Official Mud of North Dakota.

And what is it, in fact? It's Williams Soil. Any the wiser? Me neither. Wikipedia told me nothing. The US Department of Agriculture said no more than that there are 2.2 million acres of it in North Dakota (which made it a wise choice) and that it is, er, different shades of brown. It's mud, in other words. There are then 125 words explaining that the department is against discrimination "on the basis of race, color, national origin, age, disability, and where applicable, sex, marital status, familial status, parental status, religion, sexual orientation, genetic information, political beliefs, reprisal, or because all or a part of an individual's income is derived from any public assistance program." There are more words about that than about Williams Soil. But that's the thing about mud: it's dull.

There is so much of it and so few people that someone in Washington, having found the place on an atlas, picked it to stuff with nuclear missiles. It says something of how many the USA and the Soviet Union had that they agreed to *no more than* 6,000. Each. You think that was a lot? It was what they planned to have left after they'd disposed of the other 80 percent. The result is a lot of abandoned missile silos. A few are signposted as tourist attractions but most have just gone. That's why

Léo Woodland

North Dakota doesn't have an official state nuclear warhead. Just outside Cooperstown, though, it has the Ronald Reagan Minuteman Missile State Historic Site. I'm not sure Ron ever went there but the state historical society got nowhere in wringing money out of North Dakota until it offered to tack his name to it. The Republican state legislature thought that a wonderful idea and shelled out.

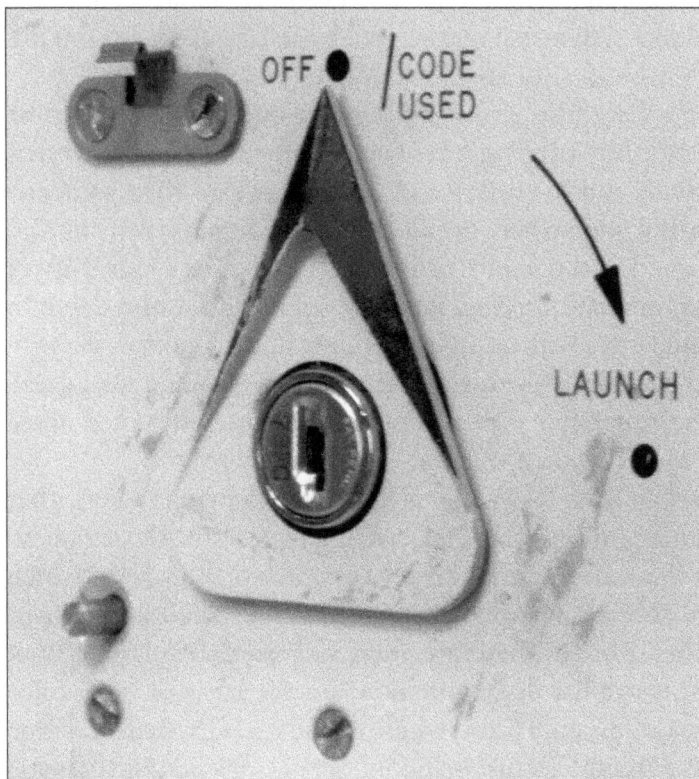

One turn and it's the end of the world.

Officially it was Oscar Zero, the November-33 control site, the underground bunker in which turning a key in a lock smaller than the one on your front door would have sent missiles whooshing out of holes all around. Nearly all these bases were destroyed as part of the treaty but the army left this one as it was on the day it walked out, hoping that one day someone else would pay to have it as a museum.

We went down. It's sometimes arcane—old paperbacks, a single public telephone with a sign asking that calls be kept short, board games and unopened corn flakes packets. Men who shared the code to shatter the world spent a day at a time underground, two at a time, hoping the call would never come. They sat at the dull gray control panel, with buttons marked Secondary Flight Monitor Control and Automatic Flight Interrogate. A black telephone had a black curly lead plugged into its face, its dial set into the control panel to the right.

The men repeatedly rehearsed what they'd do when the alarm sounded. They were to call neighboring bases to see if they too had been told to hunt about for the key they knew they'd put somewhere but couldn't quite put their hands on right now. If enough of them said they'd too been told, and if the right codes had appeared on the teleprinter, everyone went to another panel, on the left, and all at the same time they turned a key in a triangular mount marked with the chilling word "Launch."

The pressure was colossal and sleep often difficult. To pass the time, men ran repeatedly round the narrow underground corridors, closed in by the sort of heavy door you see in submarines, or discovered how high they could climb up through the girders and leave their initials. The graffiti is a human touch in a cold world. So, too, is the eight-foot fence around the surface building, which looks as harmless as a house. Local children loved hurling stones at it to set off alarms and see dozens of soldiers rush out in Jeeps.

It was all terribly secret and yet the Russians knew exactly where these centers were. For one thing, they all looked alike. And when a Russian missileer arrived to oversee the wreckage demanded by the nuclear limitation treaty, she said: "We guessed this is how your bases were and how they were linked because that's how we did it, too."

Rocket bases are still business in this part of the world. There are three of them in North Dakota, Montana and Wyoming, each with 150 nuclear missiles. Unlike the tourist sites, there are no signs, just mounds in the ground surrounded by a surprising amount of fencing.

By one of those lovely coincidences, we shared the park at Binford that night with a Pole, from Warsaw. Jan Nowicki was a gentle, gray-haired man riding from California to New York. We urged him to visit Ron's missile site, smiling and adding, "so you can see what the West had to do to stop you dropping missiles on us."

He smiled back. "The Russians, you mean. We Poles were just in everybody's way."

We all recognized it as a tease. But, seriously, we said, why not go? You'd find it interesting.

Léo Woodland

"Because I prefer the countryside," Jan said. "The world has too much of war. Especially in Poland."

Don turned up again in Pekin. Remember Don, from back in Monroeville? It was pouring to make the roads run. Pencil-smudge clouds scraped the silos. Thunder rolled. That made Pekin ideal to take refuge. For us, the weather was unfortunate. For Pekin it was disastrous. It was *en fête*. It was Pekin Day. In the park, men in waterproofs wrapped stands in gray plastic sheets. An old bus waited for visitors who looked like never coming. Paintings hung in the exhibition across the road. A woman hurried about, repeating "What a shame! What a shame!" before adding "What a shame!" somewhere else.

We splashed the length of the street in the hope of coffee. A man in a dull red plastic jacket and wet shoes directed us into the community center "if you want to get out of the rain." He was around 70 with pale blue eyes and the sort of face that looked like he'd been out in plenty of rain before. He pushed open the door and demanded four white-haired women to prepare coffee for us. They were, it has to be said, making coffee anyway, but in a way that required each to ask of the others: "Now, what can I do, dear?"

In the middle of all this, Don arrived, dripping. He was dressed as a man modeling rain clothes. He looked as though he had walked through a car wash. He had wandered into Pekin the previous day—in the dry—and been persuaded to spend the weekend and enjoy the show. Politeness demanded he stick about. Since Monroeville, he said, he had been riding shorter and shorter days, until he was now down to 30 miles. He had thought about riding in the Rockies, near Whitefish, but decided against it. That cut several days' riding off his route and left him a problem: he had a booking and a ticket for the train home. He was trying to fill the yawning time ahead of him.

"I thought I might go into the casinos on the Indian reservations," he said. "Not to gamble: just to watch other people and spend some time."

We asked why Pekin was called Pekin. Nobody knew. A tall, fair, smiling man called Rod said "Lot of odd names round here. We live down the way in a place called McVille."

We said we had seen signs for it.

"What sort of name is that?" he asked. "We live in a prefix and a suffix."

He told us the area was settled by Swedes in the late 1800s but that the region really came to life when the railway arrived in 1906. "The railroad company acquired land and then sold it to create towns that would bring them trade. And the brochures they produced! Real lavish things singing the praises of the area. They'd point out that we're on the same latitude as Paris, France… which is true, but…"

He laughed.

I knew railway companies used a lot of Chinese workers—coolees—but we couldn't decide if that was then or later. Maybe someone had commented that it was "like Pekin down there." Since there was no name for a town yet to be built, it could have stuck.

"Could be," Rod said, unconvinced but determined to sound polite.

We went on to the Sioux reservation at Warwick, in search of a drink. The reservation is a self-governing enclave which stretches from Devil's Lake. Many people refer to it as Devil's Lake reservation. The roads were gravel, the buildings flat-roofed and spaced apart. Signs were hand-painted. This, we noticed, was consistent even on police stations and administrative buildings. There was a filling station with two pickups and two white men in cowboy hats. Across the road was a bar with a plain metal door and a grill across the single window. A neon sign for Budweiser and the word "open" were just visible beyond it.

We leaned our bikes against a black, tubular rail that could have served for hitching horses and stepped towards the door. We had barely reached the handle when it opened with some force and a man with expressionless eyes seemed surprised there were two steps to street level. After him came a lively woman in pants and sweater and painted toenails, carrying a pink drink in a plastic glass.

"Oh, hello," she said. "I'm an Indian!"

Steph laughed.

"I think I worked that out," she said.

The woman looked serious.

"How's that?"

Steph pointed to her sweatshirt. "It says INDIAN. And your lovely skin tone, too."

The woman smiled, pleased.

"I never burn," she said, swirling her drink.

"I do," Steph said. She rolled back a leg of her shorts to show untanned skin beneath. The woman laughed. Her friend looked less certain, having trouble following.

"He's my cousin," the woman said. "My mother and his mother are sisters. And he's drunk. That's why I'm driving." She had trouble forming her words. "Where you guys from, anyhow?"

We explained, going through the usual variations of how to pronounce "France." The man thought he understood and said: "I got a friend in Oshkosh." It may not have been Oshkosh but when you're that drunk everywhere sounds like Oshkosh.

"You know you're on a reservation, doncha?" the woman asked. We said we did. Steph asked if she lived in Warwick. She said she didn't, slightly indignantly, as if anyone would *choose* to live there. "We live over..." She waved her arms and named somewhere we didn't catch.

"What's in your glass?" Steph asked.

"Vodka and cranberry juice. It's good. You want some?"

Steph declined. "I've got a bicycle to ride," she said, the irony unnoticed.

"Well, you met two Indians now," the woman said, slightly mysteriously—or as a statement of the obvious. She waved good-bye and they got into their car and drove down the street. Twenty minutes later they passed us on the highway with a lot of tooting and friendly waves through opened windows.

"Lovely people," Steph observed, "but I'm glad they're ahead and not behind us."

Still on the reservation, we stopped at the shop in Tokio. We had seen Pekin and Tokio on the same day. It was a small, box-like place slightly raised from the road. Outside, two women sat in a battered red car with "White power" and a swastika wiped into the dirt on the doors.

"Who did that?" I asked.

The elder woman looked surprised and said: "A deer. I hit a deer." That was no surprise. Most cars look as though they've hit deer.

"No, what's written on your car."

She got out to look. I thought she'd be angry, at least embarrassed. Instead, she shook in shrill, nervous laughter. As though she didn't know the appropriate reaction. Together, we washed it off with a wet cloth. It was the first wash the car had had in years and the brightness of the paint surprised the woman so much that she reached out and touched it.

The shop was run by a burly man I'd place in his late 20s. It had the usual central aisle and the usual heap of boxes, crates and all the rest. What made it unusual was the display of the boss's basketball trophies along two walls.

"And those are only some of them," Curtis said. "I'm too short to be a basketball player, but it's real popular round here. But what's really catching on is..." He said something like "total combat fighting" or "no-limits boxing."

"Used to do it myself for seven years," he explained, "'til the injuries got too bad." He felt the scars round his jaw.

"Looks dangerous," we said.

He felt his jaw again, trying to decide. "Well, yeah, there are refs and ambulances and stuff. Some guys don't know when to stop, though. They're only 4 ounce gloves. You get a real hard puncher and you feel his knuckles hit your jaw like he had no gloves on at all. But, yeah, guess I'm too outta shape now."

We camped in the park at Minnewaukan, a town that will soon be under water. Buildings lie empty and there is an air of dignified decay. The lake used to be 12 miles away and only two feet deep. Now it laps at houses. It is three feet from the school's gym. Classes are protected by sand bags. "No parking" signs are marooned in water that has flooded one of the exits from the village. Hoses cross sidewalks from basements to the street, emptying one but filling the other, moving the problem down the road and back to the lake. From where it seeps through land and floods the basement again. Water flows in but there is no way out.

The woman in the single store, a normally bright and happy type who was filling in for a friend at weekends, looked resigned. She brought out old photos of the town and two from more recent months. On the first, undated but probably from the 1940s, there was no water anywhere. On the second, it had drowned roads, a boat launch and fields and threatens the school.

"They've put in a curb behind the school to stop the waves eroding the ground," she said, pointing to a line on the photo, "but that won't stop the water rising. They're working on the outlet on the other side of the lake. The problem is what to do with the water. The rivers elsewhere can't take any more without flooding there as well. And there was a plan to send it to Canada, but Canada doesn't want it because they say it's too dirty. "I moved here from Wisconsin five years ago because I liked it, but now I wonder how much longer it's going to be here to enjoy. We're just too small for people to be bothered with."

A woman drove by in a white pickup. Unprompted, she wound down her window and shouted: "So sad to think nothing of this will be here next year." Next year was tricky to predict but next morning was much easier. It was Sunday and the town's old soldiers were cooking breakfast in their basement headquarters. A sign stood in the center of the busiest crossroads in town and even the most myopic could stand inches from it and read it for hours. Nothing was happening.

We walked down the metal staircase that led from the sidewalk and uncertainly in through a narrow door into the American Legion.

"*Tak*," said a man behind a table inside. He had gray hair and watery blue eyes. "It's Norwegian for 'thanks'" he added. We had just given him $14 for two full breakfasts. He added the words for "one hundred thanks" and then for "one hundred thousand thanks." I said I wasn't Garrison Keillor and that I knew only one word in Norwegian and that was *Norge*. I pronounced it *Norr-hyuh*, which may be right or may not be. I also know the words for yes, no and Oslo, but that would have been bragging.

"What's *Norr-hyuh*?" the old soldier asked. "I don't know that one."

I said it was Norwegian for Norway. It used to be on stamps I collected as a kid. "Are you from Norway?"

"No, born and bred in North Dakota. Never been to Norway in my life." Life seemed too short to ask why he was talking Norwegian. The old boy was sitting beneath a picture of George Washington. A cabinet on the wall held a rack of antique guns and a gas mask. The man cooking pancakes wore a blue hat lettered in gold to say he had fought in Korea. Some of the others wore service caps and others made do with baseball caps embroidered with the names of tractor companies. They didn't look at all ready to go to war.

"This is pretty much all we do," explained an improbably tall, smiling man with a silver beard. "Every fourth Sunday."

"But you'd be off to the trenches at a moment's notice when the call comes," I teased. He was about 70.

"When you're 18, 19, you would be," he said. "Once you've been there, you ain't so keen to get back."

Sticky Buns Across America

I asked the man with watery eyes the difference between the American Legion and the Veterans of Foreign Wars. They sometimes had rival headquarters on different sides of a town's crossroads, as if they had dug in with trenches.

"Says it pretty much in the title. You been in the military, you can join the Legion. To join the veterans, you got to have served abroad."

"Is there rivalry between the two?"

"A little, but not much. A lot of folk belong to both."

"And would they merge?"

"Can't see any reason as why they should."

"So why belong to both?"

"So's when they go to Washington, they can say they got so many members."

He told us his story, how he had been a teacher, first in the USA, then in Micronesia. His children now worked in caring professions, he said with pride. His wife died of cancer in 1976 and he'd gone to teach on an Indian reservation. I asked his opinion of reservations. We wanted to hear something good about one.

"Can't speak for now, of course, but in the eighties it was a hard place."

"To live, or to work?"

"Both."

"In what way?"

"Well, I tell you, we used to have a horse. And that was getting stolen all the time and the saddle and harness'd be taken and they'd turn the horse loose. One time the horse got hit by a car because of that."

He sighed, got up and walked the length of the room to sell more tickets.

JULY

In the United States, everybody takes an interest in everybody else. Of course, though this is wonderful, it encourages gossip and everything has to be known about everybody. America was founded by Puritans and this means that nobody should set his sights on the White House until he is so old that all the typists he ever employed (in any capacity whatsoever) are dead.

—Quentin Crisp, *Resident Alien*

5

Broken, rutted, mind-numbing pavement running from horizon to horizon over the land of god-awful distance.

The towns, the small villages, rolled by, one by one. Rugby claimed to be the geographical center of North America but wasn't. The center is 20 miles down the road and in a field, although that hasn't discouraged Rugby from erecting a marker conveniently beside its crossroads and in a café parking lot. Granville was where the people were paid $100,000 for renaming the village McGillicuddy City USA to publicize a brand of drinks. Minot, larger than the rest, paid the government $50,000 to install missile bases there. And then we were in oil country.

The long dreary path of US2 stretched on and on. William Least Heat-Moon in *Blue Highways* called it "the most desolate of the great east-west routes; it was two lanes of patched, broken, rutted, mind-numbing pavement running from horizon to horizon over the land of god-awful distance." Sometimes we had a broad shoulder, sometimes nothing. Always there was traffic: cars, trucks and giant coach-like RVs with names like Great Escape and Road Prowler, exactly what something that enormous could never be.

Do these people never ponder how much of the world's resources they use, how much pollution they are cause, how ugly they make the world, as they burn along at 10 miles to the gallon? Two people in a vehicle that would take 60. They sit like weekend admirals, drinking coffee and watching the world pass on still more television. We don't have RVs in Europe. They are too large for European roads, too expensive for European gas prices, and you'd probably need a truck or bus license to drive one. Alarmingly, we were told that, here, anyone could drive one on a car license and that licenses were handed out in Montana from the age of 14.

I picked up an old copy of *Highways*, the magazine for RV drivers. Half of page 25 was an advertisement. "New for 2009," it said in white on red. "Traveler's Guide to the Firearm Laws of the Fifty States—a state-by-state guide to the gun laws most useful to the traveler." The magazine praised: "If you carry a weapon in your rig, you need this book…"

The disturbing thing is that to many Americans this wouldn't sound at all odd.

The east and west of North Dakota couldn't be more different. The east is open, rolling, windblown. The west is all those but peppered with nodding donkeys and modern oil wells that look like rocket launchers. On the surface, tractors do tractor things and cattle graze. Two miles down, oil lies in shale. So much that people come to international conferences here. So much that it could supply half what America uses. A mayor grew excited on television as we sat in a bar. "This time the boom is here to stay," he was saying. "It's not going to go away."

Steph put down her drink and said: "I wonder if that's what they used to say in Titusville just before the oil gave out." Because it's happened before. The oil costs so much to get out that it depends on high prices. When prices fall, drillers go elsewhere. Meanwhile towns burst their sides to build new housing. Stanley was circled by inexpensive, small houses built in a hurry. Oil towns must be like the Wild West, although with less shooting—"duking it out," as Wanda put it. The effect of so many footloose men on twilight zones must be interesting.

And then families follow. Shopkeepers sell three times more and delivery trucks block the street. Doctors are overwhelmed. Schools wonder what to do with all the new children—and how to attract teachers if all the houses in town are taken. The mundane job of taxing and registering everybody has turned from a clerkish backwater to a torrent of paperwork. And it will last until the price of oil makes it uneconomic.

USA Today told us that America gave the land away long ago to encourage people to farm here. It came with ownership of all that grew on top and all that lay beneath. Some farmers still own their rights and they rent land to oil companies and collect a royalty on what's lifted. It's made some, many perhaps, millionaires. Less happy are those who collect only the rent, because those who there before them sold their rights to make ends meet during the Dust Bowl years.

It is so hard to imagine a countryside of another season, let alone another era. It took a long time to realize that notices strapped to lamp posts in even the quietest villages weren't telling residents not to park on the street overnight because the mayor wanted to keep the place tidy. It was to let snow plows get through. When you're sweating and wilting on a loaded bike, it's impossible to imagine the place knee deep in snow. Equally, it's hard now to imagine how it must have been in the Dust Bowl years, the misery, the destruction, the disaster not just of having your throat and lungs filled with dirt but in seeing all hope of even meager crops being blown who knows where.

I read a riveting book called *The Worst Hard Time*. In it, Timothy Egan wrote: "On May 9, 1934, a flock of whirlwinds started up in the northern prairie, in the Dakotas and eastern Montana, where people had fled the homesteads two decades earlier. The sun at midmorning turned orange and looked swollen. The sky seemed as if it were matted by a window screen. The next day, a mass of dust-filled clouds marched east, picking up strength as they found the jet stream winds, moving towards the population centers.

"By the time this black front hit Illinois and Ohio, the formations had merged into what looked to pilots like a solid block of airborne dirt. Planes had to fly 15,000 feet to get above it, and when they finally topped out at their ceiling, the pilots described the storm in apocalyptic terms. Carrying three tons of dust for every American alive, the formation moved over the Midwest. It covered Chicago at night, dumping an estimated six thousand tons, the dust slinking down walls as if every home and every office had sprung a leak. By morning, the dust fell like snow over Boston and Scranton, and then New York slipped under partial darkness. Now the storm was measured at 1,800 miles wide, a great rectangle of dust from the Great Plains to the Atlantic, weighing 350 million tons."

Every time it rains here, someone rushes to offer shelter. Or to say we should find some. I think the first time was in Page. We were camping in the park and not far off turning in for the night when a woman arrived in a pickup. We'd been seen in the bar, she said, where we'd been recovering from the excitement of a street auction which sold old wrenches, birdcages and 1960s car manuals for a dollar the box.

We'd been directed to the park by a man called Tom, who was also in the bar. The bar in Page doubles as the town hall. Tom wore a white T-shirt boasting "Proud to be American" and he was drinking beer—"always from a bottle, never from a can." Tom was head of opening the showers across the road at the ball park. He said he loved North Dakota and told us there were no bears there. I thought he said there were no beers, which sounded worrying.

At some time Tom had met Vicky, the woman in the pickup. The two had discussed us and the weather and the peril we were in, so *"Higher Dawn,"* Vicky called, "I was wondering how committed you are to sleeping in the park tonight." Her pickup was loaded with logs and she leaned out of its window. "Only they say there's gonna be a storm and they're talking o' hail. You may not wanna be out in that. Ain't saying it's gonna happen, but it might."

I looked at Steph, Steph looked at me and Vicky looked at both of us. A good tent will stand up to about everything but not being shotblasted by ice.

"I gotta room back of the bank I usually hire out. But you can have it. No problem."

In Culbertson, just along the road, the night had grown darker when another woman came out to spread alarm and suggest a rescue. All the towns along here offer camping in their parks and generally showers as well. In Culbertson, they are at the swimming pool a short ride away. After a couple of days without a shower, we stood under the hot water and significantly reduced the chance of spreading pestilence across the continent. At about 11, when all was dark and silent—America goes to bed early—a woman from a neighboring house flashed a light on the tent and shouted: "There's a storm coming—take in your washing and check in at the motel up the road. My husband drives an oil tanker and he's just called me from 30 miles away to say they got 60 mph winds up there."

Well, I started up the road to check the motel and Steph began clearing the tent. Then I realized I didn't know where the motel was and we both realized that if all it was going to do was blow, then we might as well stay where we were. The tent wasn't going to blow anywhere with us inside it. And it had withstood gales on mountain tops in the Pyrenees.

In time, there was thunder and then eventually there was driving rain. The tent shook.

"Hi, you in there!" a voice shouted above the noise of nature. A man this time. "You OK in there?"

We were so OK that we were both asleep. Steph, faster to realize what was happening, yelled back: "We're fine."

"What?"

"We're fine."

"Can't hear you."

She began trying to work out the thousand or so zippers and fasteners that it takes to open the door, then decided that she didn't care to anyway.

"We're OK, thanks."

This time the man heard.

"Well, we're in the trailer just alongside. You change your mind, you can come in with us."

"Thanks, but we're OK in here," Steph answered.

"OK, then. Well, you know where we are. You have a safe night."

We found out in the morning—although with what accuracy, we never knew—that an inch of rain had fallen. There were puddles around the Canadian trailer halfway up the park. We saw the man who had been so determined to rescue us and we thanked him.

"You got wet, too," we said.

"Just a little." There was irony in his voice. We got the impression that his wife had sent him out in the rain and that words had been said afterwards. The wife never appeared.

When people speak of the bleak, featureless reaches of North Dakota, they mean the bleak, featureless reaches of Montana. It's not easy to tell the two states apart, except for the fact that Montana is flatter and duller. *Eastern* Montana. Gary Griffeth, who like us was riding across the country but with his wife following in a camper-van, said he wondered why people who lived in western Montana, or went there a lot, so often fell silent when he mentioned eastern Montana. It was as though he had mentioned a pedophile relative. Now, he said, he understood.

Indians had precious little luck in the development of America. This is where loads of them were put. Our first hour in Montana was along what locals called "the Indian road", which here means any road that passes through a reservation. It was heaven after US2 and it passed through interesting cliffs of tortured, melting orange rock. The few drivers raised a languid finger from the wheel in salute. Police cars here don't say POLICE on them; they say COPS.

We were on the Fort Peck reservation, our largest yet. The shallow hills were covered by green scrub. There were no fences. Indians never had fences. White men had those. If there were cattle, they still roamed as they did in the days of the Plains from which the first residents were driven. The houses were modest, a single story with small windows, painted gray or dull blue. Any sense that each stood on a surveyed plot was muted. Signs were all hand painted. Two gray wooden posts by the road supported white signs about 18 inches by 30. The edges were bounded by wavery black, green, blue, yellow and red stripes. The message, black on white above the sort of design, in the same colors, you might see on a campfire blanket, said:

June 24–27
Dancers, Campers, Singers
Welcome to the 37th Annual
BADLAND POW-WOW

I thought powwows were, or used to be, discreet gatherings of tribal elders to, er, powwow. It turns out they are vast jamborees attracting people from far around, many of whom accept that they wouldn't willingly be on Indian land any other time, and which fill every hotel from here to Kansas. But they are little lights in a gloomy night.

In Brockton we pulled into the village on the unusual promise of finding a café, a laundry, a casino and a video library all in the same room. And sure enough it was there, a squat white building of plastic slats made to look like wood. The sign above the door and the ice cabinet, a legally obligatory fixture in America, read:

B and S	Enjoy	Broasted
Laundry	Coca-Cola	Chicken

Inside were a chubby, friendly woman who knew everybody and a sullen, fatter older woman who stared at the slot machines that constitute casinos here. Forget any notion about roulette wheels and urbane croupiers. (For some reason, people criticize Indians for living off gambling. I often wondered if they had the same disdain for the

House of Monaco or ever flew to Las Vegas.) Across the road was the equally squat post office. Inside was a man you just knew liked cats and had a way with soft furnishings.

"Well, *Higher Dawn*, folks," he said. "Welcome to Brockton now."

He wasn't Indian. He did live on a reservation, though, further down the road in Poplar. We talked about the world and our role within it and then we pointed to the old chap sitting at a bench outside the café-laundry-casino, to whom we'd nodded on the way past.

"Oh, Jim," said the postmaster. "Lovely guy. Loves talking to folks."

Jim looked up sleepily. He took off his blue cap and dropped it on the wooden table. He had a full head of bristled gray hair, four or five days of stubble, eyes that stayed all but closed from a lifetime in the sun, and a face like a partly squashed orange. He wore a red and blue patterned shirt with buttoned pockets. He was 88, he told us.

"I just sit here biding my time. Stops me watching too much television," he said in a kindly voice. He was born on the reservation and he had never left, he said. "Used to run the Standard Oil gas station cross the way." He swept his hand in a vague gesture. "Ran it for 42 years. Then when Standard pulled out, the man who owned the building tried coming to a deal but that never worked out."

His wife had been diabetic. That led to gangrene in her toes and finally to amputation of both legs below the knee. "She died a while back, so I been by myself since then."

"And has the reservation changed since you were a boy?"

"Have I changed?"

"No, has Brockton changed?"

"Oh, completely."

"For better or worse?"

"For worse. Too much drink and drugs here now. Used to be only old men drank. Now it's the kids, too. And drugs. And they go about smashing windows and breaking into cars."

"Why do they do that?"

"Ain't nothing for them to do."

"Can't they work?"

"There's no work here. Farmers employ some o' them but not otherwise."

"So where do they get the money for drink and drugs?"

"Well, government's got a program. If you're looking for work and you can't find anything, you get help from the government. But they got to take a drugs test before they qualify for that, so a lot of them fail then."

We were going in circles. If those who took drugs couldn't get money, then where did the money come to get drugs? There was a touch of old-timer's disease here, a belief that the world had gone to the dogs.

"Would you ever live anywhere else?"

"I'd love to live somewhere else."

"Off the reservation?"

"Off the reservation. But the problem's the same in all these towns round here. I thought about moving to Williston, but that's the same. Full of oil men. That's who brought the drugs in if you ask me. They call me Crazy Horse here, you know that?"

I smiled.

"Ain't my name but I go in there…" He gestured at the café. "They all say 'Hi, Crazy Horse.'"

"People still have those old Indian names?"

"Sure do."

"And if your name was Crazy Horse, what would people call you? They couldn't call you Crazy, surely?"

"Just Crazy Horse, I guess."

"And 'Mr. Horse'?"

"No, Crazy Horse."

I picked up the *Fort Peck Journal*, "an independent voice of the Fort Peck Reservation," $1. There were lots of people in there with good Indian names. On the cover was a practical-looking man with a warm face and a thick, short beard and mustache. "Welding instructor Keith Red Elk hands out certificates of completion at their graduation last Fri., July 10," the caption said. Next to the picture was a story bylined "Bonnie Red Elk, Journal Editor." On page five was an advertisement "remembering Winifred Violet Red Eagle Smith."

The paper's leader was moving. The editor wrote:

Needs must be prioritized

A growing family lives in a small, dilapidated trailer on the east end of Poplar. They have a houseful of children and teens. The floor of the trailer is so weak that the mother-in-law refuses to come and visit. In fact, when the woman of the house was cooking at her stove, she went through the floor. In the winter, blankets hang over a thin window that is cracked and broken. They have to use the cook stove's oven to help heat the trailer…

It's almost incomprehensible that a family has to live in such horrific conditions in this day and age. If this was a family with council connections, would this be allowed? We (the Fort Peck Tribes) have a Fort Peck Housing Authority, a tribal program, that seems to have scads of money for delegations and to create new positions. The Tribes have money to send elders on culturally related trips, and donate to youth groups.

Our tribal leaders need to prioritize. Our leaders need to make sure the needs of the neediest are met. After all, they are the only ones who can do it, and that's why they were elected.

There was an espresso bar disguised as a coffee pot beside the road in Poplar. Two riders coming the other way, a father and son, said they weren't stopping because the town gave them "bad vibes." I'm not surprised: account after account calls it Stab City. Or says that other people call it Stab City. If you don't get stabbed, your bike, your kit, probably even the shoes on your feet will disappear. But nobody knows who this happens to. I sent a message to the paper's editor but there was no answer.

Just beyond the coffee pot café was the old tribal jail. It's a shallow, ochre-colored place with bars on its few upright windows and again in the door. A wagon wheel and a seriously peeling red bench stood outside. On the same grounds were the remains of the Poplar ferry. It looked like a two-story wooden hut nailed to a flat-topped barge. A chain from its interior turned a paddle wheel set across the stern, the whole lot in the same decaying white paint. It seemed symptomatic that it was called *Poplar Pride* and that the sign explaining that pride was so rotten and peeling that it was hard to read.

The jail is now a museum. On the wall was an explanation easier on the eyes. It said the *Poplar Pride* was one of the last ferries on the Missouri. It saw water in 1949 and sailed until June 1969, a year after a bridge was finished. The cutting said: "Sailing faithfully across the Missouri River on an average of 376 crossings each month, the *Pride* ran during the day, from April through November. A man and wife couple operated the boat the last few years and the *Pride* can boast she was unique in that sometimes she broke water with a woman at the helm. Miles of distance between Poplar and the South Side were shortened because of the ferry. To cattlemen during calving, she meant the difference between livelihood and disaster. To the people who were sick, she meant hope and sometimes even life. She served us well."

The town bought it rather than see it broken up. But it stands unprotected in the weather, uncared for and rotting.

We so much wanted to hear something good of Indian reservations. We talked with Aola, a wrinkle-faced woman of 79, smiling, her lips painted red, her short gray hair parted boyishly above the left eye. She breathed with the help of transparent tubes that ran from her nose to an oxygen bottle the size of a coffee flask by her hip. It made a gurgling noise. She was an Assiniboine Indian, aware that the reservation is dominated by Sioux. She said there was no rivalry but the fact that she mentioned it showed that there was.

"I grew up in Indiana," she said, sitting behind the museum's small counter and waiting for anyone else to come in. A mannequin Indian with his feathers trailing to his backside—"he was an important guy with that many feathers"—stood silently in one of the cells. Another cell had a hole where an inmate had tried to dig a way out. A more peaceful inmate had painted a color portrait of an Indian with a single feather and a flopping pigtail on his shoulder.

"My mother brought me up as a White." She said it with more disdain than she'd shown for the Sioux.

"Why did she do that?"

"Because she knew about reservation life."

Aola met a man on a visit to Fort Peck. She was 18 and she fell instantly in love. He was a Sioux, incidentally.

"When the time came to go, my mother said we were leaving and I said if she was leaving then she was leaving without me. So she left in tears and my boyfriend and I, we got an old van and we chased her as far as Culbertson, but we never caught her. I got married a few weeks later, though she did send me a beautiful dress to get married."

Aola confirmed what Jim, "Crazy Horse", had said: that there was no work and, worse, no hope. "I carry on working and I'll carry on until I'm 100 because I don't want to be like the others."

"Meaning...?"

"That they get up in the morning and go looking for a bottle. And they don't care how they live, what their houses are like."

I thought of that editorial in the paper. And I asked how people lived.

"Off benefits, largely. I'd say there's only 15 percent who've got a job. Government pays you if you've got children at home or if you're looking for a job. The government distributes food. Some people go there and use it but some, they take it and sell it."

"Do you get more benefits because you're Indian and living on a reservation?"

"No. Same as anyone else in Montana."

"Some people have said you get more."

"No. Just the same."

"There's an oil boom down the road in Stanley and Williston. Is there no work there?"

She shrugged as if to say "yes, but they won't go." Then she said: "There could be an oil boom here. That's our oil they're drilling there. The way the land lies, the oil here flows down to Williston. They could drill for it here but they're... I nearly said a word there!"

She said she received $10 a week to welcome visitors to the museum. "That barely pays the groceries for a day at home, but..."

What she meant was that it kept her active. It meant she was needed. She contributed something and, beyond that, she had pride. And pride is what Fort Peck lacked.

Montana grew worse and worse. So did the wind. Bike-shop legend says America should be ridden from west to east, because that is the way the wind blew. We were going east to west, because that's the way history went and because it put the Rockies and the Pacific at the end. To have gloried in the Rockies and then spent a month counting fence posts across Montana would be like having a dollar and dropping it down a drain.

As for the wind, that had been behind us, pretty much day after day since the Great Lakes. You need some sort of agenda on a ride like this, a timetable, or you'll get to the end with two weeks to kick your heels or, possibly worse, you'll realize on the last morning that there are still 250 kilometers between you and your plane. We envied Americans who said they'd just get to the other end and catch a train home. We did have time in hand, thanks to the tail winds earlier, but we weren't about to squander them if the wind continued to torment us across the Plains.

The problem was lack of roads. America is not a place to find detailed road maps easily. When you do, you have to trust that all the roads it shows have hard tops. A great many don't. Worse, it varies between states. Every side road was surfaced in Ohio but out here very few were. We didn't have the time or the ability to choose. We stayed on US2, the road that grew with the railroad beside it.

We stopped for July 4, America's national holiday, when we got to Glasgow. Nothing happened in Glasgow except for evening fireworks a bit too far away to be worth seeing. Do the people who plan these things not realize that tired cyclists go to bed around 9pm!

Glasgow is quite the regional town, with more than 3,000 people. Hinsdale, "Home of The Raiders" and the next place down the US2, has all of… Well, write to "Jack" and the mail man will get your letter there. Get the picture?

We did in fact meet Jack. We were in the little shop there that has a couple of tables to facilitate the downing of Sticky Buns. Hinsdale, it turned out, had had a street parade and a band and everything else a foreigner hopes to see on July 4. The cheerful woman behind the counter said there were 200 people in Hinsdale and that she knew them all. Jack said he had lived there 10 years and knows most, "or, at least, I know who they belong to." He's retired now—he worked for the gas company down the road in Saco for 30 years—but he still "runs some cattle." When I asked how many he was slightly elusive and said: "I dunno—30, maybe 40," as though it were something a man might forget. "Get other ranchers to look after them now, though."

"Beef cattle?"

"All o'them. Kids round here, they think milk comes out of a bottle."

He spoke slowly, his mouth wide, his eyes half-closed and smiling, his head topped with a Panama hat with a crumpled rim. He nodded when the woman added: "This is a proper community. You address a letter just to 'Jack' and it'll find the right person. If not first go then the third or fourth. Write 'Mr. Jack' or 'the mayor' and it'll go straight there."

"You the mayor?" we asked.

"That's what they call me but we're not an incorporated village, so we don't have a mayor. But one day I was mouthing off and I said or someone said I should be mayor. And I knew some guys who'd be my town council. It was just a joke but the nickname stuck." He took another slow mouthful of coffee from a golden waxed plastic cup.

"And what do you do now? Sit here and drink coffee all day?"

He laughed.

"Good deal more than I oughta," he said, a man who talks without urgency and moves with not much more.

"And how do you cope with mosquitoes when you live here?" We had been warned that Glasgow, Hinsdale and above all Saco were Mosquito Alley. They flew in swarms and showed no mercy. I don't know what's in Deet, which is what shops sold, but it kept them off. Unfortunately it also melted the back of my cycling jersey, reducing the Lycra to its underlying netting. I was wondering how much further I could ride dressed in a butterfly net.

Jack smiled and pushed back the tip of his hat with a finger.

"You don't cope. You just put up with them. When I was working in the fields, you just wear a hat with a net tucked into your shirt, and you keep everything buttoned up. But you can't get by them. You mightn't think you're too lucky, going inta the wind the way it's blowing, but that's a blessing. Wind keeps the mosquitoes down and they can't feed and they die."

He smiled and he hit a favorite thought. "Those hoodlums," he said, "they oughta strip them naked and peg them out on the ground a while. Them mosquitoes'll get 'em and they wouldn't bother anyone again for a while."

"So we're lucky, fighting into this wind, then?"

"Yep. Don't mean they're no more mosquitoes, though. They lay their eggs deep down. While back, some university fellas, they took some of the gumbo to test back in their *labba-tory* some place. That was still hatchin' mosskeeters next seven years."

We'll say this for Montana: it has an entertaining way of explaining its history. Every couple of hours we passed a black, lettered board hanging from a wooden frame. They were written with dry humor. Take this one for instance:

Léo Woodland

EARLY DAY OUTLAWS

The old West produced some tolerably lurid gangsters. Their hole card was a single-action frontier model .45 Colt, and their long suit was fanning it a split second faster than similarly inclined gents. This talent sometimes postponed their obsequies quite a while, providing they weren't pushed into taking up rope spinning from the loop end of a lariat by a wearied public. Through choice or force of circumstances these parties sometimes threw in with the "wild bunch"—rough riding, shooting hombres, prone to disregard the customary respect accorded other people's cattle brands.

Kid Curry's stomping ground in the 1880s was the Little Rockies country about 40 miles southwest of here. On July 3, 1901, Curry and his partners, Butch Cassidy, the Sundance Kid, and Deaf Charlie, pulled off a premature Independence Day celebration by holding up the Great Northern Railway's No. 3 passenger train and blowing up the express car safe near this point. Montana's most famous train robbery netted the crooks a bag of gold coins and $40,000 in unsigned and worthless banknotes. Soon after, Curry and his gang departed Montana.

It's funny how signs like this make history come alive. I'd never heard of the Sundance Kid or Butch Cassidy until the film. And now we were peering at the line where they struck. We saw the little blue and white station at Malta, too, where the raid started, although some reports say Cassidy wasn't there. The train pulled in at 1:30pm, several men boarded and one climbed in approved style along the roof of the cars until he reached the locomotive. There he ordered the engineer to stop where the sign stands now, where Deaf Charlie was waiting with horses and dynamite.

They disconnected the baggage van, fired several shots down the train to discourage heads from poking out, then blew the safe. It took them three goes. They took the "eight hundred sheets with four notes on each being three ten-dollar and one twenty-dollar bills," all worthless,

$500, a bolt of green silk fabric, a package of watches and a bag of coins. They scampered and spent the money. The bills were traced. One man was arrested in St. Louis. Another was killed by detectives while on a drunken spree at Flo Williams' whorehouse in San Antonio. Another was captured, got 20 years' hard labor and then escaped. A year later he robbed another train and committed suicide in the shoot-out that followed.

And the Sundance Kid? He rode off into the sunset as any self-respecting bank robber should. For the rest, it was a short life being a bandit but it didn't lack color.

You can't—or at any rate you shouldn't—crawl along the roof of a train unless it's traveling slowly. They don't go so very fast now but then they went far slower. Bill Bryson recounted: "Cars were connected by nothing more sophisticated than chains, so that they were constantly shunting into one another, jarring the hapless occupants. Front-facing passengers had the choice of sitting with the windows closed—not an attractive option in hot weather—or suffering the assault of hot cinders, jocularly called 'eyedrops', that blew in a steady stream back from the locomotive.

"Fires, derailments and breakdowns were constant possibilities, and until late in the 19th century even the food was a positive hazard. Until 1868 when a new word and phenomenon entered the language—the dining-car—customers were permitted to detrain at way stations and given 20 minutes to throw a meal down their gullets. The proprietors of these often remote and Godforsaken outposts offered what food they could get their hands on—or, more often, get away with. Diners at Sidney, Nebraska, were routinely fed what most presumed to be chicken stew; in fact, its basic component was prairie dog. Some said they were lucky to get that."

The trains went rarely more than 20 miles per hour yet they swallowed coal and water. Word says most towns here along the so-called Hi-Line of the north are there only because locomotives couldn't manage more than 15 miles without needing more water. And then, because they stopped, farmers brought grain to ship further along the line. And so were born the giant silos that are the first sign you're actually moving. It takes an hour to ride from one to the other, more with a headwind, but at least there's hope.

Léo Woodland

The line was the dream of a magnate called James Hill. Getting people to go out and work in the heat of summer and the snow of winter—remember, "The interesting thing about the weather here is that at any time of the year, it can kill you"—meant Hill couldn't be too fussy. It's quite something, then, to learn that he reached what is now Havre—pronounced *Havva*—and, in the words of the town guide, found "many people of dubious quality settled in the bottom [river valley] and ran bars and brothels out of cottonwood cabins and tents. It was such a tough town that James J. Hill threatened to pull his railroad out."

For four generations the word *road* meant *railway*. What are now called roads were then *trails*. Remember the man directing us to "the hard road." But trains now use diesel fuel to power electric motors. They don't stop at stations any more. Day after day we saw entire trains of Chinese containers, trains that took minutes to pass and stretched for a mile. "Just look at one and you see why the America economy is changing," a man told us in Dodson. And, with it, the whole Hi-Line. It is dying.

The man in Dodson, where we paused for a drink, owned what had once been a store and a separate restaurant. The restaurant had closed and there were now a couple of tables in the shop, which didn't look much healthier. He looked up from the meal he was eating on the only other table, asked about our ride without much interest and then, more earnestly, asked: "Why don't you folks give up this traveling and come and settle down in Dodson?"

Like everywhere along US2, Dodson needed new blood. The grain elevators, monarchs of the plains, keep towns alive. That and a couple of other employers now and then. But they are waiting for the tumbleweed. The bars in Dodson, and there were a surprising number, have closed. So had everything else we saw. Young people can't find work. When they go, there's nobody left to attract business. It's a vicious circle.

"All we got living here now is seniors," the man said.

Whose fault is it? Blame the politicians. That was Keith's message in Keith's Kafe, in Joplin. He had bright, dark eyes below neatly parted silver hair and above a long shaggy gray beard that fell across his chest and hid the words "Rabbit Hunter" on his white T-shirt. "Fella in ZZ Top, his is the same but his is thicker, I guess," he said.

The map showed Joplin had somewhere to drink and, with no great conviction, we set off up the slope, across the railway tracks and on to a dust road. And there, on the corner, was Keith, his beard and the café that he has been trying for a long time to sell. Joplin is another place that stands in the shadow of silos, hooted at by every Burlington, Northern and Santa Fe that pulls through. The population has halved in the 16 years that Keith has been there. Around a hundred cling on. Joplin was like Dodson, but Dodson was at least on the highway. You didn't need a map to know it was there.

"Course," Keith protested, "this president of ours ain't helping matters much, giving shitpots o' tax money to people who won't work." Not there but elsewhere we had seen signs pinned to trees urging that Barack Obama should be impeached. A car license plate had N 0 BAMA on it. Keith made no protest when I suggested he was, perhaps, a Republican. "I own guns, I hunt and I kill animals," he answered with a smile, as though that were as good a definition as any.

Folk leave because there's no work and, because people leave, work doesn't come. I put it like that but Keith, a man who has thought about life and now pronounces on it, insisted: "There *is* work. Or there could be. Trouble is people round here can't see further than farming. Politicians round here don't have imagination. Some way from here, I saw someone started a place handling straw. Maybe makes electricity by burning straw. Now that's the kind of small business that would go well all around here. No point in hoping some big employer is going to come in and save everything. But they lack imagination. Take Chester down the road. They had some money and what did they do with it? They built a swimming pool. That's not going to bring in work. That's a plaything!"

He asked if we had met Jim, who'd taken over the bar at Fresno, or at any rate near the turning to Fresno dam. We said we had, that we had found it unexpectedly and with some pleasure after setting off from Chester. Jim was a Londoner who had lived in the States for 21 years, first in California and then in Colorado, in Denver. He was sitting in the middle of the big drinking area, changing his boots, when we arrived.

"I came over here to see my wife's folks and this place is on the market and so we bought it, just like that," he said, sorting out a wrinkle in his socks and pulling the second boot into place. "It was in a real mess when we got it and we've just been sorting it out ever since." Ever since meant for the last six weeks. He said the people down the road in Kremlin—nobody knows how the village got the name—packed the bar for the Fourth of July.

"Wish he'd known about me," Keith said. "I been trying to sell this place for years. I'm sick of it, to tell you the truth. It pays me a living but then I don't ask much. Had a little shop alongside and that could be opened again as well. He'd o'been better off being here in a village instead of out there by the road. It's always the same, when you're new, people come and see you. It's what happens after six months that counts. That's when things change."

We didn't say but we rather hoped Jim would succeed. He seemed a nice guy. When we went to pay, he insisted the coffees were on the house and refused to hear more. We thought he was Australian at first. Mix a strong London accent—he was born in the center, in Southwark, "although I could have been born on an Italian liner, because my mother only just made it back from Australia in time"—with American and you get Australian.

"I get on the phone to my old friends for half an hour," he said, "and the accent comes back and my wife can't understand me." A Southwark accent—it's pronounced *Suth'ck*—is, shall we say, quite strong.

By now, we wished we'd gone another way. Out of Montana, for instance. Or at any rate well to the south. We could have gone down through Missoula. We could, to be honest, as happily have gone down through Mexico. The worst of the traffic had turned off, it's true, heading for interstates. But even train drivers found it boring. It's become a game to wave at trains and for engineers to hoot back. They're looking for cyclists and cyclists can hardly miss the trains.

Freight drivers were the most bored. As well they might be, the slow pace at which they travel. There can be three locomotives in the front, bright orange with yellow stripes, BNSF in huge capitals, and another behind. It takes five minutes to get up to speed. Engineers of passenger trains are more snooty. Or perhaps they have more to do. We became such experts on the *Empire Builder* that we could predict when it would pass. It's the sole passenger train on the route—the only one we ever saw, anyway—and, while it goes at a leisurely average of 50 miles per hour across America, stops included, it looks sleek with its gray cars lined in blue. It starts in Chicago and goes to Seattle or Portland, depending which end of the train you sit in. On the way it passes through Illinois, Wisconsin, Minnesota, North Dakota, Montana, Idaho, Washington and Oregon. Half a million people take it every year; at times we envied them.

Sticky Buns Across America

Of course, if we *had* caught the train, we'd have missed the town that built a life—and a brothel—underground and the town that had such pretensions that it held the world heavyweight boxing championship. And things like that were just why we had come to America. That and Sticky Buns in neon-lit gas stations.

Havre was where the railroad man found the residents so excitable that he thought about taking his trains elsewhere. Things were bad when he arrived but they soon grow worse. Even the *Havre Daily News* acknowledged that. Among those arriving on the new trains "were a vast assortment of characters seeking to profit from the newly created communities and their residents. C. W. 'Shorty' Young was one such character, who arrived on the train in 1894 without money enough even to pay for a haircut. Soon, by catering to people's vices, Young was to become one of the wealthiest men in Havre.

"Havre's isolation, lack of law enforcement and population of railroaders, soldiers, miners and cowboys were a volatile mixture and Havre soon gained a reputation as the rowdiest town in the West. It was not uncommon to see numerous fights, some including knives and guns, on Havre's city streets. Hill [the railroad entrepreneur] himself is said to have threatened to pull his railroad terminal out of Havre after paying a visit with a group of investors he wanted to impress. In the short walk through town, Hill is said to have witnessed six drunken fights in broad daylight. The name 'red light district' is said to have evolved from the train crews' habit of hanging their red lanterns outside the doors of a prostitute's crib they happened to be visiting."

And how did the city come to live underground? Because in 1904 a lot of the wooden buildings burned down. Preachers said the town had become the new Sodom, punished by heaven for its loose ways. But loose ways have an appeal and, to get over the lack of timber with which to rebuild, people opened the passages that ran from basement to basement and turned those into the town instead. And fitted them—Shorty Young *oblige*—with a brothel, bars and an opium den.

Well, times change and the railroad that proved the town's undoing became its salvation. Lumber was brought in and the town moved back to street level. The subterranean passages closed and filled with junk and rats. People knew they were there but they belonged to the past. And then, in 1990, two local men and a bunch of volunteers set about shifting the remains of much of a century, opening corridors, creating rooms, restoring and equipping those that remained. They found as much original material as they could, although some of what's now underground was never there at the time, and created a good picture of how it must have been. It's for tourists, of course, the guided tour. But we were tourists and so we bought a ticket and went down. Pleased we did, too.

Not much to see in Shelby, though, given its bigger role in history. In fact there's nothing left to see. Ride out of town to the west and you may just notice a small electricity station, a pizza restaurant, a motel and a gas station, all in a line on the left. In the distance is a bridge across the road. Well, it was here that Shelby held the world heavyweight boxing championship.

There are 3,200 people in Shelby these days. They've made it a pleasant place and we stopped for mixed coffee and ice cream and then, outside, chatted with two women intrigued by our loaded bikes. It was a town to feel at ease in. Should you think to drill a hole right through the Earth's center, it would come out in a town in French Antarctica. In Port-aux-Français, probably, because that seems to be the only place there. And why's that so astonishing? Because—well, OK, I admit it's not *that* astonishing—Shelby is one of only three cities in the USA which has a built-up area on exactly the other side of the world. You're going to ask me where the other two are, which prompts an excellent moment to expose my ignorance.

I'll tell you, though, that one of the men who began the Genome Project—Leroy Hood—was born in Shelby. And that the heavyweight boxing championship was in 1923, when the town was only two-thirds the size. The story goes back to the railroad. Shelby found oil in 1922, the only place in Montana to have it, and it felt pretty good about itself. The trouble was that no one had heard of the place. Rectify that and they would come flocking on the train and bring their money and turn Shelby into a boom town. The problem was how to do it. A man with the gangster-like name of James "The Body" Johnson realized he had the answer the day he read that Montreal had offered $100,000 to put on a fight between Jack Dempsey and a challenger not yet named.

Johnson was a fan—he adored Dempsey—and he owned a lot of surrounding land. There were no television networks so fans would have to come to Shelby. If they then bought land to strike oil, he would grow rich without the sweat of prospecting and digging. Shelby offered $300,000, put up by banks who thrilled to the idea of countless local oil millionaires. Johnson picked July the Fourth in the hope that patriotism would loosen wallets. Such was the optimism that temporary hotels went up and an octagonal stadium the size of a football field was built on a farm.

Shelby paid in installments but it couldn't come up with the last $100,000. Fans canceled their tickets. By the time the fight was on again, it was too late to sell tickets and get people to town. Only a handful sat in a stadium designed for 42,000. The organizers panicked and lowered the price from $25 to $10. Some paid but thousands more pushed over the barbed wire and barged in. The stadium filled with locals seeing a championship boxing match for nothing and the promoters and the banks got none of their money. Four banks went out of business, including the one owned by James Johnson's father. The stadium was sold as scrap. There are historical markers in Montana for less significant events but not a mention of the day Shelby had ambitions beyond its reach.

For the fourth time, we crossed the border, this time ridding ourselves at last of US2 and riding north into a gale. Canadian air came rushing at us with eye-watering, lung-filling enthusiasm. We crawled at 8 miles per hour, thinking Zen-like thoughts and hoping for the best. This was the price to pay for the tail wind we had enjoyed for the last month: a wind that slapped our faces and wearied our bodies and sapped our spirit. A wind that turned whenever we turned, always to face us. We looked like being out there a long time.

This was always going to be one of the hardest days, not because it was so hilly but because the entire 120 kilometers promised not a single dependable shop or a cafe. We knew about the little store across the border at Del Bonita but we knew too that an old lady ran it and that it opened only irregularly. There was nothing but Del Bonita all along the dogleg to the Mormon town of Cardston. Not a village nor even a collection of houses. It was to be the wildest, emptiest countryside of the journey. All, at any rate, but for a strange moment.

Throughout, the road rose and dropped and rose again, finally topping 1,300 meters and bringing our first good view of the Rockies.

Léo Woodland

The countryside here was smooth rolls and mountains. The fields were sown, cropped and sometimes plowed. There were beef cattle here and there. The land was rounded and white patches showed through the grass and crops. Wind and rain had worn the underlying white soil and a loaf-shaped outcrop the size of a cathedral was called Chalk Butte to underline the theory. The wind still blew but less now that the sun had risen properly. In midmorning we crossed with a guy who had ridden 70 miles since breakfast and hadn't realized he had a gale pressing his back wheel.

The border between the United States and Canada is the longest straight line in the world. The result is that you can't predict where it will fall. Most borders are at the tops of hills or the bottoms of valleys, or they follow roads or skirt forests. Not this one. Although here, just before Del Bonita, it happens to be at the top of a hill. We puffed our way up it and rode past the little border building on the left, on the American side. Nobody looked, still less came out. American borders are all about those going in, not those leaving, which makes you wonder where the figures come from for immigrants who've outstayed their time.

There were several hundred yards before the road took half a step to the right to pass the Canadian control. That attractive red and white Canadian flag with its maple leaf was out horizontally in the wind. On the right, in no man's land, three dozen people were enjoying burgers and drinks around a table beside an RV. Chairs had been set into a horseshoe and, the folk being older rather than younger, we took it for a school reunion or a pensioners' outing. We forgot that we were in no man's land, neither in the USA or Canada. We didn't, however, forget that we were hungry. And that was where a trim, blond woman in jeans, black T-shirt and glasses saved us. She ran into the road and waved to us with a smile.

"Come and have a burger with us!" No words could have been more welcome.

"Well, gladly, but who are you?"

"The Flying Farmers…"

Well, if you have never heard of them you're not alone. We hadn't either. But the name said it all, in that they were farmers from both sides of the border who flew. Their planes were lined up on both sides of a grass runway that stretched at a right angle from the road. There are neither as many farmers nor as many flyers as there were. Membership is therefore fairly liberal. Young farmers don't have the same interest in private aviation and they don't have the money. Older farmers have the money and the planes but they no longer farm.

I looked up the Flying Farmers' website and it said: "Of all private pilots, Flying Farmers are perhaps the only ones who will tell you their Cessnas and Beechcrafts and Pipers are no different from their combines, tractors, and pickup trucks. After all, airplanes are workhorses too, for hauling supplies, for checking irrigation systems, for compressing the time between the farm and parts store." A woman with sun-wrinkled skin whispered to us that the only farm work they did was a couple of trips a year to inspect cattle "but that's enough to justify putting the plane down as a tax expense."

Well, they couldn't have been more hospitable. Margot, our hijacker, introduced us to her family and members pushed drink and food on us. A man whose name I didn't catch said: "We come from Canada and the US and this is the only place we can meet without going abroad. The runway goes straight down the border in no man's land. Look and you'll see all the Canadian planes are lined up on the Canadian side and all the Americans are on the other.

"Twenty years ago this strip was built, but it's in better condition than ever. I don't recall we've ever replaced the grass. All we do is fill in the gopher holes."

It emerged later that there were more planes of one nationality than the other and that the border guards, who would normally have demanded passports and documentation but seemed bemused by the whole thing—they came along for burgers as well—had turned a blind eye to the temporary export of aircraft from one side to the other. It had never occurred to either of us that flying from one country to the other demanded the pilot call ahead and then land at a checkpoint that has an airstrip. There he has to show his passport and fill in forms.

"You pilots are pretty good at remembering to bring your passports," a woman guard from the Canadian side said in a speech. "It's people in cars who give us problems." No mention of bicycles, although we hadn't reached the Canadian side yet.

We left in a gap between the speeches, having been introduced to everybody. Margot came running after us as we walked round the tables and hamburger stands to get to our bikes. "Here," she said, "I've packed you some cookies to help you through the rest of the journey." We rode away into the village, turned left by the little shop—which was closed—and ran with the wind down and down and down, the Rockies coming nearer and the sky growing black. We rode into Cardston between two storms, a corridor between heaps of black cloud. The rain caught us as we pulled up at a motel.

Cardston is an alcohol-free town where three in four people are Mormons. Spending Sunday there was never going to be exciting. All but a hidden supermarket closed on Saturday afternoon and a dinosaur could have walked through the city next day without anybody's noticing.

Cardston is predominantly Mormon because it was founded by Charles Card, an American who thought it best to slip over the border when the US spotted he had more than the conventional number of wives. His house, a timber cottage with a tiled roof set back from the road behind a grass garden, is in the main street. Alongside it is a mural of the Card family crossing the plains in a covered wagon in 1856. We walked up to the mausoleum-like stone temple that overlooks the town, a heavy, dramatic building behind a six-sided lawn fenced by a shallow stone wall and, more significantly, behind a pale green metal gate. Beside the gate was an office with a small display of artifacts in its depth. Two impossibly sweet women in their late 60s gushed over us so inoffensively that it became offensive. It was like being doused in perfume and fed marshmallow.

"May we go inside?"

"Oh, no," said the older woman, taken aback but sticking to her smile. "Oh, no, you can't go in."

We didn't like to ask why. It hadn't occurred to us that people who stand on your doorstep in neat suits and bring you the good word, brother, would do anything but *drag* us inside. We said nothing and hoped she would explain. In such inoffensive company, it seemed impolite to ask. But she said nothing. The other woman sensed the moment and said: "You must be very healthy to make such a long journey." And that was that. We could look round pictures of out-of-focus people wielding shovels and modern pictures of digging machinery at work, but that was it. Maybe Mormons look like Mormons. Maybe they make secret signs, like Freemasons. Maybe *nobody* was allowed inside. We never found out.

Sticky Buns Across America

We paid for our unheavenly intrusion, however. And how. The wind rose and rose. We had our day off, counting the cigarette ends and beer cans in the Fay Wray fountain (Fay Wray was the blonde who wriggled in the grasp of King Kong in the film posters and who lived briefly in town), then set off next day. And turned round next day. The gale shrieked at us, each gust bringing us close to a halt, each mile to our destination becoming increasingly unattainable.

"What do you think?" Steph shouted from behind me.

"Eh?"

"Do you think we're going to make it?"

I didn't think we were, any more than she did, but we'd barely left town. The road rose slightly ahead of us and dropped out of sight. Maybe it would be better in open country—triumph of desperation over logic—and perhaps we would be saved by the gentle descent. It wasn't and we weren't. It was worse than ever. We looked at each other. Words weren't needed. Nor were the brakes. We just stopped pedaling and the bikes stopped dead. Little is less suited to fighting a headwind than a bike surrounded by four bags. It takes on the aerodynamic sleekness of a barn door.

Well, we had time in hand. Being pushed across Minnesota and North Dakota had seen to that. This was no time to be the unknown soldier. We set off again, turned in the road and rode back into town at three times the speed limit. That afternoon Cindy, the woman who ran the camp site from an RV parked across from the reception office, came across as our rebuilt tent rattled in the blast. She was "seriously worried" about us. Hail "the size of golf balls "(bad hail is always "the size of golf balls") had fallen on the Calgary Stampede.

"We have a four-bedroom house just out of town," she shrieked above the gale. "Why don't you go and sleep there? There's nobody there."

Why didn't we? Really because we were dispirited by riding out of town earlier. The thought of packing the tent and starting again, and then maybe of not being able to rise before dawn to escape, we hoped, the next day's blast, was too much. Once more we assured her that the tent had withstood worse than this, that it was made for worse than this. I hoped she wasn't looking when I fought its flapping expanses to turn it more into the wind, losing tent pegs in the process, taking down the tent again to find them, struggling again to rebuild our shelter.

Léo Woodland

The wind rose still more. Next to arrive was the woman's husband. "That's gonna get to a hundred K, the wind," he said. "Think about our offer." We asked what the forecast had been for Cardston. Had anyone spoken of hail? Violent wind is rarely a problem and rain never is. But hail can shred a tent in minutes. There was no hail forecast. We stayed put and an hour later the wind dropped to a breeze.

Next morning we rose in a light frost before dawn to get going before the gale rose again. It soon did. Men have won medals for less than we did that day. I have a 24-tooth inner chainring and I used it endlessly, even on the flat. If gobbledygook means nothing to you, imagine putting your car into its lowest gear and leaving it there. The wind rose and rose. It was enough just to keep going against it. To fight would have been disastrous. When it was dead ahead, we made slow progress, little faster than walking. When the road turned, we leaned against it like dying trees. The wind blew me off the road three times in five minutes, happily on to gravel to the right. When it pushed the other side, the struggle was a physical and nervous battle to avoid being pushed—unexpectedly so far as less observant drivers were concerned—into traffic from behind.

Birds had given up flying.

Steph said: "I kept finding my front wheel pushed about. You can't stay as far to one side as you want because of the risk of overcompensating and running off the road. It was mentally exhausting, just keeping the bike straight, not daring to take a hand off the bars to drink or blow your nose."

The compensation was the Rockies. Yesterday they were a smudge. It was astonishing how quickly they became reality, ahead and beside us. They were austere and treeless, occasional streaks of snow where the sun had been kept out of a crevice or stream bed. The slopes were sudden, bald and brown.

Relief came, in a way, when after several hours we turned left on to a lesser road into Waterton Lake National Park. Now the wind was less against us but more unpredictable. The mountain edges sent it swirling, like a drunk bouncing round a bar, and the conifers beside the road held back the wind and then let it through in rushes. The road rose to 1,700 meters, a long, slow and alarmingly zigzag until after who knows how long it swung left and the gale below without inhibition at our backs. It blew us helter-skelter into the flat, glacial valley. We rushed through the little Blood Tribe Indian reservation, a small and so far as we could see uninhabited annex to the larger reservation near Cardston, then on towards Chief Mountain, the flat-topped giant which Indians revere. It stands pot-shaped and flat-topped amid all the peaks and gashes of lesser mountains. It was the first feature of the Rockies we saw, when they were a gray hint on the horizon. It was astonishing how that little smudge turned so quickly into the remains of one of the greatest eruptions the world has known.

The valley was green, flat, with trees on both sides. The mountains gazed contemptuous of those who defied nature. There were small, dark lakes with dancing white sheep where the wind whipped them. Black clouds shrugged their shoulders above the peaks. To be stuck back at height with a storm raging and nowhere to pitch a tent was less than attractive. The ride back into America could wait for the morning.

"Sir, don't take a picture of me."

The man with the camera hesitated. He was 10 yards inside American territory. He lowered his camera to just below his chin, uncertain because the demand—a demand rather than a request—had surprised him.

"Sir, I said DON'T take my picture."

The border guard was angry now. He was certain the camera that had clicked. He walked determinedly to the motorcyclist standing in black leathers beside his parked machine.

"Show me the camera," he commanded.

"I was just taking a picture of my buddies coming through over there," he protested, pointing to eight or nine other motorcyclists waiting to enter the country.

"Show me the pictures you've taken," the guard repeated, taking no notice. The motorcyclist pushed buttons and showed him the pictures that appeared on the screen on the back of his camera. The guard went through them as far as he chose. And then, seeing that there were indeed no pictures of him, he handed back the camera without an apology but with a polite "Thank you, sir." In pre-digital days, presumably, the film would have been stripped from the camera. But then maybe in pre-digital days there wasn't the same fear that has pervaded the USA since the World Trade Center air crashes.

Léo Woodland

We were received nothing but cheerfully when we passed through borders. In Canada they were amused, in America they were amused but they were also wary in a friendly way. The border guards smiled and made pleasant conversation but their eyes never left us. Every movement was being judged. We had 10-year visas. Mine was like anybody else's but the issuing clerk in Paris had been so astonished when Steph explained why she wanted to visit for more than three months that he wrote on it in capitals: "During 2010: will make cross-country cycling trip across USA. But visa not limited to this trip: good for others."

"Jeez, where'd they write that?" the woman inspecting our passports gasped. "Never seen anything like that before." She called her colleague, the one who grew upset with the motorcyclist, and they marveled together. And then one of them asked where we'd come into the US.

"Rouses Point," Steph said.

"Where's that?" They were trying to make out the number code that the control had printed on our $6 ticket. "South of Montreal," Steph said. "New York state."

They looked again. But that—quoting whatever the number was—that's us, they said. Or if it wasn't them—I forget now—it was a border control just a bit further across the mountains. And "mountains" is the relevant word because in early May, when we first entered the States, mountain roads were closed by snow and the entry points hadn't opened. Such is the confusion that computers and numbered lists can generate.

It used to be that to get into the US you had to be looked up in a huge book. That's how it was when I first went, at the end of the 1970s. It took some minutes to be checked because the book was eight inches thick and contained thousands of names of the sort that confused immigration authorities at Ellis Island. I don't know about then but later you had to answer a questionnaire which asked:

- Are you a member of the Third Reich?
- Do you plan to overthrow the US government?
- Are you an international money launderer?

You may think I'm joking. I'm not. Those were the questions, among others, that the form asked. I talked about it once to the man sitting next to me. He said he had asked the immigration man in New York whether anyone ever wrote "Yes."

"The man just looked at me very seriously and said 'Sir, if they do, we don't let them in.' I could never decide whether he was being very dry or very stupid."

"I do so hope that this Going to the Sun road is going to be worth it after all this," Steph shivered. It was little more than freezing as we rode away

Going to the Sun, and to the top of Logan Pass, at more than 2,000 meters..

from the border, preceded by a bear. And she was right because we have ridden three sides round a square and on every day there has been a 50 kilometer per hour wind against us. We struggled on against the wind and groaned at the relentless lack of taste of St. Mary's, the last town before Glacier National Park. It is as though everyone who hoped to fry food, sell trinkets and generally make the most of tourists struck an invisible wall and heaped up there. But the cost of entering the park was immediately repaid, not in cash but in relief from commercialization and in the panorama of sheer rock against billowing green grass. St. Mary Lake lay beyond the grass, deep in its valley, its dark, clear water showing its teeth in the wind.

It was afternoon and the traffic was constant and the road narrow. But a theme linked us all. There was an air of *bon enfant*, of getting along. Nobody hurried because to hurry was to bring the pleasure to a speedier end. We were allowed time and space to ride slowly into the wind. And we rode four miles, that's all, as far as the first camp site. The sign said it was full but we were directed to the sloping and wooded triangle of the hiker-biker section. A jolly volunteer warden said: "You find space where you can. We never turn away a hiker or a biker. We're just too respectful of what you guys do."

Next morning she was back at six, as ebullient as ever but now concerned. We had been up for half an hour. Everyone else was asleep. Some of the hikers had talked late into the night, despite Steph's pleas for them not to, and I was tempted to clatter our pots noisily outside their tents. It was the arrival of the warden that discouraged me.

"Have you seen a bear?" she asked.

We said we hadn't. Not since the previous day and several hours' riding back, anyway.

"Someone reported that a bear just walked through the hiker-biker section."

I kept to myself the regret that it hadn't broken into the hikers' tents and eaten them. In fact a few days later a bear did indeed break in on campers, although some distance away, and it had killed one. The *Billings Gazette* said a man had been killed and two women injured: "Paige and Don Wilhelm, of Aledo, Texas, heard a scream at about 1:30am. At first, they thought it was just teenagers screwing around. Then they heard another scream, this one closer. 'I heard somebody yell, Stop! No!' said Paige Wilhelm. And then they heard the woman yell: 'A bear's attacked me!' They drove through the campground, honking their horn to scare the bear while trying to find help, they said. That's when they came across another victim, a young man, who'd been bitten in the calf and managed to scare the animal off by punching it in the head. The man killed was about a quarter-mile west of where the other campers were attacked. He was camping alone."

State park camp grounds have solid, bear-proof lockers with recessed handles. Bears would quickly learn a conventional handle. The rule is to put in all you have that could smell of food: pots and pans, of course, food itself but also shaving cream, soap and bike bags. The American Bear Association says: "There is perhaps no other animal with a keener sense of smell. Bears rely on their sense of smell to locate mates, detect and avoid danger in the form of other bears and humans, identify cubs, and find food. The area of nasal mucous membrane in a bear's head is 100 times larger than in a human's. This gives a bear a sense of smell that is seven times greater than a bloodhound's. A black bear in California was once seen to travel upwind three miles in a straight line to reach the carcass of a dead deer."

The good news is that bears rarely see humans as prey and attack only when surprised, provoked or separated from their young. The problems come when a bear learns that humans are tasty. The advice we've been given is to stay in our car should we see one…

Going to the Sun is the prettiest name a road could have. The scenery is reputed to match it. For us it was once a distant highlight, a landmark in a long ride. Now we were closer to the Pacific than the Atlantic, the ride was closing and people were more impressed by where we'd been than where we were going. There was a strong feeling of being in the Northwest.

The story is common to religions. Local Indians had fallen on hard times. They were poor, dispirited and hungry. Then a wise man told them how to live a better, happier life. The people thought the world of him but he set off back through the hills from which he'd come and walked into the setting sun, never to appear again. The Indians said he had gone to the sun and gave the name to the mountain on which the sun set.

How that came to be the formal name is less certain. The *Glacier Gazette* started its explanation with "As the story goes…", a good sign that nobody actually knew. But, "as the story goes, writer James Willard Schultz and a Blackfeet friend coined the name 'Going to the Sun'. While butchering a ram on a high road, the two discussed that the peak would make an ideal spot for a vision quest. The two arrived at the title for one of the most famous roads in the United States."

If, like me, you wonder what a "vision quest" might be, send your letter to the *Glacier Gazette*. This, after all, is a paper that can write "discussed that the peak would make" without embarrassment. James Schultz is less doubtful, though. He was an author and an explorer who lived with the Pikuni tribe in the late 1800s. They called him Spotted Robe. On that basis I should be named Food-Splattered Sweater.

Anyway, miners "acquired" the area from the Blackfeet in 1895 and dug for gold. Nobody else went there because the best you could do was get off the train at Belton (now West Glacier), take a stagecoach to Lake McDonald and then a boat to the Snyder Hotel. There you collapsed on your bed too exhausted for dinner. There was debate about turning a near-impossible mule track into a tourist road. For centuries nobody wanted to go into the mountains. Now that people saw the beauty and not the timber and minerals they might provide, they weren't sure about defacing the place with a road. But unless they built a road they couldn't see what they had preserved. It's the eternal conundrum.

It was locals who won. A businessman in Kalispell wrote to the *Gazette*: "A park without roads is a menace to civilization and settlement and a barrier to communication between states and districts." The wilderness was to be "civilized." Bids opened in 1925 and the pass was completed in 1932, starting from the west. It took 300 men and 250 tons of explosive. Boring the tunnel on the east took a day to move five feet. The gradient much of the way was six percent because 1930s cars had to shift to second on anything steeper. We shifted down as well but, quite honestly, the climb wasn't as hard as we'd been told. "It's our version of Alpe d'Huez," someone had warned. But it isn't. It was only on the gravel of a mile of roadworks that we got into bottom gear.

We left just after dawn, to avoid the wind and to get started before the sightseers in cars and RVs. The road rose just gently, empty, damp, cut into a ledge between a corrugated, vertical wall of brown stone and, beneath us, the dawn blue of St. Mary Lake. Shadows lay across the mountains across the water, sometimes covering streaks of snow that lay in crevices the sun never penetrated, never hiding the bonnet-like snow on the peaks. Nobody else was on the road.

Going to the Sun Mountain passed on our right, the road steeper now, the wind held back by cold stone walls of rock. Outcrops lay by the road, projected in the massive collision that caused the Rockies, striated like broken wood. Moss lay on their flat tops and foliage on their sides. Daisy-like flowers grew at their foot. Clouds thickened as we rose slowly towards them. Shadows fell. Everything became sinister, imposing rather than pretty. "Striking" would be a good word. For a long half an hour it seemed we would be deprived of this beautiful road. But ahead, the clouds parted over the summit. Blue sky lay ahead. We couldn't be sure but the other side could meet its reputation for having better weather.

A road like this demands constant maintenance. It is under snow much of the year. The group led by the young beanpole had only a week earlier sat out a day at its base, hoping the road would clear for them to ride from the west. It never did. The road menders must have moved in as soon as they could, perhaps even before the snow had gone. The warning signs were out long before we neared the top and red lights sent the now steady traffic first one way and then the other. It took three people to operate the lights at our end of the works, one with a radio, one walking up and down the lines of waiting cars, the third doing nothing obvious.

And then the third found a job. She looked into the open hood of a pickup printed with the name of a contracting company. And she screamed. The other two ran to her side. She held one hand over her mouth and pointed into the pickup's engine with the other.

"There's a marmot in there!"

It's not every day you see a marmot in a car engine, so we joined the crowd. And there it was, behind all those boxes and tubes you can't identify in modern cars these days because they don't make them like they used to back when you could see what everything did and you didn't have to go running down to the garage to get the slightest job done and then they present you with this enormous bill and you say it's no wonder that weasel-eyed guy down there always looks so pleased with himself the money he must be making.

"How long you had that hood open, Chuck [or Hank or Dude or some other American name]?"

Chuck, Hank and Dude walked over, scratched his head, said "I dunno, maybe jus' five minutes," and everyone began discussing not only why a marmot might have climbed into the engine compartment but how and how long ago had it happened. Had it been there when Chuck drove down to town and back again?

Meanwhile the walkie-talkie was saying "*Got a gap here, guys, you wanna send me a few?*" and nobody was taking any notice. They were more occupied with how to get the marmot out. Saying "Here, coochie-coochie-coochie" did nothing but make the marmot snarl and hiss and bare its rodent teeth. We stood around for a while and I took a picture, not because it helped but because that's what you do as a sightseer. And then finally Chuck, Hank and Dude said he had an idea and to hang on, and he walked back to where he had been signaling traffic, picked up his flag, turned it backwards in his hand, wedged it down behind the marmot and shoehorned it out. It moved surprisingly fast, jumped over the side of the car and ran in a bad mood down the mountain, over the edge of the road and into the undergrowth.

"Darned if I seen anything like that before," Chuck, Hank and Dude said. We hadn't either, we said. The walkie-talkie was shouting "*Hey,*

What every good motor needs: it's very own marmot

you guys there or you fallen asleep maybe?" and normal service resumed. We dropped in behind the cars and pickups and crawled through the roadworks so slowly, given the unmade road and the gradient, that there was already a hefty line waiting to come the other way when we reached the distant lights.

From there we were just moments from the top, passing a distant frozen waterfall to our left and banks of dirty snow to our right. We stopped at the tourist center and joined the other thousand or so people who'd gone there and wondered why they'd bothered. We muscled three Japanese girls from in front of the sign announcing we had crested Logan Pass at 2,025 meters and took each other's picture. To the girls we said we had to be down the other side before the road closed to cyclists. They looked at us as though they hadn't understood, which doubtless they hadn't, but in the face of dominant people dressed in bright Lycra they felt it best to surrender their place.

6

Doncha get kinda scared that someone will come and drop somethin' on your head while you're in that liddle tent?

In theory you should be able to go all the way from Logan Pass to the Pacific without once going uphill. If you stuck to the river, you could. It is, after all, the watershed. Americans are very taken by the continental divide and put up signs whenever they can. On a bike, it is not at all possible to reach the Pacific by freewheeling all the way, although there is a gloriously long drop from the pass to the bank of Lake McDonald. And there we had to stop. Not because we'd ridden far enough but because signs told us we had to. Cyclists have to be off the road much of the day so as not to annoy people sitting in RVs.

There is an odd relationship between cyclists and other road-users in the USA. Most drivers are amazingly courteous. They'll drive to the other side of the road if they can to accommodate you. They often smile and wave encouragement. What makes the relationship between cyclists and their roads ambiguous is that cyclists are expected to use the shoulder, the emergency parking strip, and not the highway. There isn't a strip on lesser roads, of course, and it's there that drivers show most consideration. But sometimes there isn't one on big roads, or as in North Dakota and Montana it can be narrow or filled with rumble strip. And then, when you ride on the road as a consequence, it baffles and even annoys drivers. That is when they came too close and when we grew aware of how many RV drivers left their steps down, creating scythes like Boadicea's chariot.

Sometimes fellow bikies recommended routes not for their scenery but "because there's a good shoulder." In Britain, this sort of thing provoked a battle that started in 1930 and is only resolving itself now. Road planners provided paths beside roads less for the convenience of cyclists—because the paths were poor, rarely maintained and often used for parking—but to improve the lot of drivers. The paths weren't compulsory—making sure of that was another battle—but there was an angry assumption that cyclists should use them. At least they should be grateful for facilities built at public expense, as though that argument didn't apply to roads as well.

So, the argument went, use paths and more will be built. And built dangerously because they increased the junctions and side roads that a cyclist had to negotiate. Using them was a step to making them compulsory and driving cyclists off the road entirely. That was a threat in the 1950s and 1960s. As the authors of *The Penguin Book of the Bicycle* wrote, a target study of one town in 1963 "showed that 17 percent of trips to work were made by bicycle, compared with 36 percent on foot or using public transport. [The consultant] recommended that £4½ million be spent on urban motorways, but he decided that it would have been 'very expensive, and probably impracticable, to build a completely separate system of tracks for bicycles.'"

America is still undecided which way to blow the dominos. A few cities treat cyclists commendably. Quite a few more are in the British 1950s, building paths beside the road but forcing cyclists to cross side roads they wouldn't have had to cross on the highway. Most don't know what to do, or think like Colin Buchanan, the English consultant. Nothing is more insensitive—stupid would be better—than to expect cyclists on busy highways to use the side strip and then make it narrow and fill half of what's left with rumble strip. Why not put the corrugations to the left, on the drivers' side? But that would make the road six inches narrower for RV drivers, wouldn't it?

I remembered, as I wrote that, a curious conversation in Nashua, where a café has become a favorite simply because it is there and because North Dakota can be a windy place. We got into conversation with the waitress, a bright-eyed girl in her teens. Like Wanda and Craig in Hitterdal, she had seen a lot of cyclists come through but she'd never known why. Again, we explained that she was on a cross-country bike route, that we were riding from Montreal to the Pacific and that we had maps showing us how to do much of it on minor roads. Further along the restaurant, in another row of tables, a short, plump, dark-haired man and his wife were listening in.

"See you guys on the road," he said.

I said there were a lot of us about.

"Don't understand summin, though: why don't you guys ride on interstates? Gotta be better. Got a big shoulder on those things 'stead of them iddy-biddy things you got on the roads you ride."

An interstate was, I said, the very last place I'd ride. Forget that it may be illegal. Just think of the noise, the fumes, the monotony. I wanted to explain that it was the journey that counted on a bike. Sometimes by lunch you couldn't remember where you'd started and the place you'd spend the night hadn't been decided. And that was in a straight line. Cyclists, I wanted to say, often go round a loop, ending where they started, just for the ride, for the scenery. In a car, or pulling a trailer like he was, it's the destination that matters. It's where you get out from behind the wheel, and if you want that to happen as little as possible, you drive on interstates.

He looked unimpressed. And then he asked:

"Camp by the roadside, do ya?"

We said we didn't. He either didn't listen or didn't care.

"Doncha get kinda scared that someone will come and drop somethin' on your head while you're in that liddle tent?"

"Does that happen a lot?"

"Does what happen?"

"Do people drop things on campers' heads a lot?" He looked momentarily more stupid than ever and thought that, no, perhaps it didn't happen so frequently. "Rather sleep in my own car, though," he said. "Got your own bedroom with ya if you gotta car."

Sometimes minds never meet.

Primary-color commercialism laps the other gate to the national park as well. It was as though bad taste had held its breath for 43 miles and burst out in one enormous gasp. This was a last chance of hamburger and fries before facing the monotony of driving 43 miles through unadulterated countryside. There were tourist shops, helicopter tours, rafting companies and hotels. A miasma of fat hung above the street. I won't be so hypocritical as to deny we bought food at the supermarket but we were happy to move on.

Léo Woodland

The *Glacier Gazette* helped again at Columbia Falls. "The town certainly was home to some of the most entrepreneurial spirits of the day," it chuckled. "Local businessmen sent a steam ship up the North Fork river in search of coal deposits; the ill-fated expedition ended when the ship capsized and the crew had to walk out of the wilderness." The town then turned to religion in gratitude. I have never seen a place with so many boards listing the Ten Commandments. Maybe they covet each other's ox a lot there.

What I coveted was the old steam engine. I am more taken by old locos than oxen. This one, black with two steam domes and a high chimney, stood in an unremarkable road beside rail tracks. It had "1" painted on the smoke box door in white. The cab was built of timbers. The hidden pistons were vertical rather than horizontal and visible; Loco 1 moved by turning cogs against the driving wheels. It ran on coal or wood.

Loco 1—"Shay"—was built in 1904 to haul flatbeds of timber along the Swan valley. It moved at 12 miles per hour and in time the pace of life overtook it and it retired. A company in South America asked about buying it but lost interest when it heard it ran on standard rather than narrow-gauge rails. And then the engine rotted and rusted until Montana celebrated its centennial in 1964, the loco's 60th birthday, and volunteers set to work.

The excellently named *Hungry Horse News* explained: "Men of the community became weekend railroad laborers, carrying ties and rails, pounding spikes to complete the 300 feet of railway between the Great Northern spur and the two rails where the Shay now stands. On October 6, 1963, after much preparation, the Great Northern Railroad train master out of Whitefish gave orders to Engineer Ozzie Schmechel and Fireman Paul Reagan and Conductor F. F. 'Abe' Bronson to tow the Shay from Stoltze Land and Lumber Company at Half Moon on to Columbia Falls siding. Schmechel remembers: 'We coupled on to it and pulled it out going about five miles an hour so it wouldn't run hot. It had set so long the pads that held the grease were old and hard.'"

It is a rule of local papers to get as many names into the paper as possible. The *Hungry Horse News* didn't neglect its duty. Every volunteer who wandered by was named. And it went further: "Workers were served hot coffee and lunch by Half Moon ladies with Candy Geer, Susan Gulick, Mrs. Gary Preston, Mrs. Don Davall, Mrs. Bob Higson, Karen Beagle and Postmaster Dudley Greene assisting. As darkness stopped activity, Adrian Gill showed up with more refreshments." I worked long enough on local weeklies to know that every single person named would have bought a copy of the paper. It's small-town life throughout the world.

Leaving Columbia Falls gave us a chance to ask a gaggle of riders if they'd seen Sam. They said they hadn't. But then one remembered a camp site a day back. And there someone had spoken of a Frenchman he'd met earlier that day. Sam was still a day ahead of us.

Traffic was heavy leaving Columbia Falls but the shoulder was broad enough to close our ears and ignore it. We turned off after a while, anyway, into a road that offered itself to the right at the top of a rise. We moved from the Flathead valley—Hungry Horse is on its other bank—into the Whitefish valley to bowl into the vaguely Wild West town of Whitefish on a route followed only by cyclists. There was no other traffic.

Whitefish, like everywhere here, grew with the railway. The Northern is celebrated the length of Montana. Business are named after it and there are variations of its orange circle and black lettering in every town. So many trees fell in the town's construction that its first name was Stumptown. It's acknowledged in the names of shops and other fripperies. Pretty soon people decided Stumptown didn't do the place justice and they changed to Whitefish. I ought to know why, but I don't. The place is known for its Ding-Dong Ordinance, a rule that children had to be off the street by the time the town bell rang 9pm. That was extended to 10pm and then abandoned, not because parents or children objected but, of all things, for health and safety. The bell was beside the fire station. For decades the firemen were volunteers. They raced over at the first wisp of smoke and went off in a threnody of sirens and bells. Fire engines and police cars in America don't hold back when it comes to noise.

Then the firemen became full time. They slept in the fire station. Or tried to. They'd just nod off and this wretched bell would clang at 10pm. Firemen are sensitive and nervous men. And so a charming tradition ended.

We settled down for a long stretch on US93 beside the railroad and the Stillwater. We don't recommend this road during the week. It is peaceful on Sunday but it is narrow all week. It is an obvious secondary route to the Rockies for RVs and trailers. American trailers are no more caravans as we know them in Europe than RVs are camper vans. They are on steroids. They have grown and grown and pump themselves up when they stop and bits emerge from the sides. An American trailer is an RV without a cab, a space left for a pickup driver to reverse into, fasten hauling gear and move out. There is a pecking order in this world of get-away-from-it-all-by-taking-it-all-with-you warriors. Pulling a trailer doesn't cut it with the real RV crowd.

US93 is also a trucking road. Truckers don't drive much on Sunday. To be a cycle-tourist in the USA is to have strong views on logging trucks. We were spared that but there was still slightly less road for the traffic than we would have preferred. It skipped up and down gentle hills, the wind still in our face, between woods and past dirt turnings that led to who knows where. Someone had amused himself by stenciling a yellow diamond marked RANGE CATTLE so that it warned of STRANGE CATTLE. The sign had seven bullet marks.

To the left, before Dickey Lake, a small road led to Stryker. It had no significance other than a place to eat sandwiches. We took the gentle slope over the railway and continued along the trail of dust and compressed stone into a half-world of inexpensive wooden housing, trailers and abandoned buildings. Shabby, one-story houses were scattered like a child's toys. The few streets had names but little stood there. The white, box-like post office was clean and neat but it opened only a few hours a day. On Saturdays it opened at 7:30 and closed at 9. The postmaster went from village to village, opened a couple of hours in each, and so on through the day.

We sat in the shade of a porch of a dark, wooden home which could have been empty for years. There was no furniture and the rooms had that untidiness which remains when folk take almost everything with them. What little is left fills more than a lifetime's possessions had taken. The enigma was a white, plastic coffee machine on a window sill. Across the road, a derelict wooden house at right angles to the road. An armchair stood on the verandah like a dog pining for a dead master. An outdoor lavatory, doorless and surrounded by long grass, stood to one side.

Stryker was once a railway town, said a man in his 40s, tanned, his shirt unbuttoned to show a belly like a galleon. He had been coming and going, busying himself in a way that let him keep an eye on strangers.

"Had a depot once but that's all been mechanized now. All there is to do here now is watch the mail van come and go and count the trains," he said in a surprisingly soft voice.

All countries have high and low points, contradictions that prove quick judgments are unwise. America's is the contrast between films of wonderfully coiffed women and slim-waisted, square-jawed men living in ease in the richest country in the world—"as if everything on telly were real," as Lois, the newspaper editor, said in Monroeville—and small townships with dirt roads, a past and no future. They were built for a purpose but never enough purpose that anyone ever laid tar. Like many like it, in the 21st century, Stryker turns to mud in winter and dust in summer. And nobody we spoke to thought it odd.

Soon it may have not even a post office. That looked likely to shut. Our new friend pointed to the house with the porch where we had eaten our sandwiches and explained the coffee-maker. "They only just moved in yesterday," he said. "I ain't had a chance to meet them yet." But who'd move to Stryker?

Life is more exciting at Libby Dam. Not that you'd know it from the bored and droning women who showed us around. For one thing, the operators are always being sued by somebody or other. And second, the dam is apparently high on the list of terrorists' plans to cause mayhem and disaster. The first, from the women's resigned seriousness, seems true. The second seems less likely. In any event, terrorists who might think to toss a bomb over the side are discouraged by the need to buy a ticket. You may think I am being frivolous but until the Twin Tower air crashes, anybody could stroll across. It was the shortest way from one bank of Lake Koocanusa to the other. Now you can do it only if you have a ticket and join a group escorted by a guide who, I have to say, seemed in no physical shape to hold off a snail.

We rode beside Lake Koocanusa for half a day. It wasn't a road to take without water because the lake was always far below, down a steep embankment. Its joy is that there is no commercialism. There's nothing. The road on the other side was quiet enough but we could have held a picnic on our forestry road. A car an hour, that's all we saw, although we paid for the solitude with repeated climbing and descending.

Lake Koocanusa stretches 90 miles from British Columbia down to the dam outside Libby. Like most dams, it is no more than a wall with a hole in it. The bored guides didn't pretend it was more than that and their drawl wouldn't have convinced us anyway. It generates electricity but its main purpose is to stop flooding. The water rose and killed so many people in the late 1940s that the time had come to tame the menace and the dam went up. Or eventually it did. It took a decade to negotiate with Canada, which would also be flooded. The Canadians approved after the Americans said they would build hydroelectric dams up there as well.

The walls were laid a section at a time, starting from the main highway on the other side. Everything came in by rail and trains ended up running through a hole left in the dam. "We didn't want a dam with a hole in it,"—a rare flash of dry wit—"so we moved the railroad and built a tunnel that's the second longest in the USA."

Anything that saves lives, generates electricity and is very big cannot fail to attract an American president. Sure enough, Richard Nixon turned up to shift the first tub of cement to close the hole. The problem was that he arrived an hour late and the concrete had started to set. He needed two others to join him in tugging the rope. By the time the dam was finished, Nixon had fallen from grace and Gerald Ford had taken over.

"After the experience with Richard Nixon, we learned our lesson," the guide said. Specifically, that presidents can manage a nation and influence a world but shouldn't be trusted with anything simple. Nobody asked Ford to shift a bucket. They built him an impressive quadrant lever and set it in a frame to make it look still better. Ford and someone almost as important put a hand apiece on the lever in 1975 and pulled it towards them, supposedly starting the generators to light half a state. The reality was that the lever did no more than light a flashlight down in the control room, the signal to an unseen man in shirt sleeves to do the job properly.

The dam has upset people ever since. The water's too high, too low, too warm, too cold. The Army Corps of Engineers, who run it and see off terrorists, are always being taken to court. The person who should *really* complain is Alice Beers of Rexford. She entered a competition to give the lake a name. She chose Koocanusa because it combined letters from the Kootenai river, Canada and USA. She must have been very proud. Then the water rose and flooded her house. She had to be found somewhere else to live.

Libby, by the way, was another town on its knees. It was more impressively religious than even Columbia Falls. That had billboards reciting the Ten Commandments but Libby had all those and more and more churches than I've seen outside the Bible Belt. They lined the road going into town and they lined it leaving again in the morning. They should take note, though, that "The wages of sin is death" lacks in the grammar department.

It was odd to feel, yet again, that we were nearing the Pacific. By cycle-touring standards, we were merely scratching the surface, of course. Josie Dew once came across a man who spent his time riding from one Olympic Games to the next, not to see the running and jumping but to give him a destination. Four years, of course, gave him plenty of time to get there and therefore lots of chance for diversions. He'd been doing it since the days of gladiators. Similarly, an acquaintance called Jacques Sirat once gave himself two years to ride round the world and enjoyed it so much that he kept going. The day came when he crossed with an Australian, also riding a bike. The two talked of things of which cyclists talk and pretty soon the Australian asked: "How long ya bin on the road, then?"

To which Jacques metaphorically huffed on his finger nails and polished them on his chest and said: "Five years. 'Ow about you?"

He said the Australian gazed back without emotion and said: "Twenny-seven years."

He was, he said, locked in orbit. All he could do was keep going, keep going. There was nowhere he could call home and there was nothing he could offer an employer. He was locked in orbit.

By contrast, we had crossed, or almost crossed, a single continent. We were leaving Montana at last—we will grant you that the smaller western section is better than the east—for a brief turn in Idaho before entering Washington. Our last state. Individual states meant less to us than to Americans. But they were a way of totting our progress, another chance to take our picture, looking weary and drawn, beside a border post.

We crossed the Pend Oreille from Newport into Oldtown. After the mangling of Mille Lacs into *Milly Lacks*, we'd expected Pend Oreille to be *Ponderelly*. But no, the pronunciation was faithful to the name that

Léo Woodland

French explorers gave the local Kalispell Indians, who hung jewelry from their ears. Having passed that test, the locals named the waterside town as a compromise of French and English: Ponderay. But it's still authentic and we were oddly pleased.

Pend Oreille lake in the morning sun—our extra hour thanks to the clock change that comes every month on a bike—was still quiet enough to cast a perfect reflection of the world. Pines admire their picture in the water. What little moved on earth moved faithfully in the reflection as well. Not even fish dared to spoil the harmony. More than you can say of the navy, which used the lake to train submariners in the second world war and apparently uses it still because its depth gives acoustics similar to an ocean.

Beyond the lake, we stopped at another dying village. There are so many of them. Businesses were shut or shutting. The hotel had a grand French name and a load of scaffolding outside but it wasn't clear if it was being stripped or reopened. Two adjoining shops had been knocked into a car wash. The internet café had closed and the gas station beside the railway no longer had staff. Only a white-fronted café beside the fire station seemed open. It had become the social center of a community which lacked one.

"*Higher Dawn*," a smiling white-haired man asked as he towed in a smaller, more timid man. He too had gray hair. Both were in their seventies. "They treating you all right here this morning?" the first man asked. "If not, we may just go off down the road." He said it deliberately loud enough for everyone to hear. The oldest of the waitresses looked up. She was late twenties, early thirties, with short dark hair shaped around her face.

"Here's trouble," she said. "Double trouble."

The livelier man looked amused and hurt.

"Every morning I tell her how good she's looking," he protested. It produced an air of amused resignation in the waitress.

"I notice she hasn't said the same about you," I said.

He smiled. "She's my niece," he said.

"Is that true?", Steph asked. The girl said it was, making out she had no choice but accept it.

The two men ate their meal and then argued good-naturedly over who was going to pay the bill. "I ain't got no money for the tip," the smaller one said. "So I'll pay for the meals and you can pay the tip, because I can't afford the tip." The meals, of course, cost far more than the tip. Their lovely bout of illogicality, deliberate, was familiar to them, the product of a lifelong, small-town friendship.

"I'm on a dump run," Smiley said, turning in his seat to look over his shoulder at us. "All the family's come over to celebrate my mother-in-law's birthday. Ninety-eight, she is. Gotta clear up now. Got the truck out there." He gestured through the window. He asked intelligent questions about our trip, described the countryside we'd see, then said that he'd never been a cyclist but that he had a friend in his 50s who had tried—"Thought there couldn't be anything much to cycling. That's what he said. So he went to Switzerland with some friends. Every picture we saw of him on the internet, he was pushing his bike. After that I don't think he did any more."

He, his friend and his pickup passed us as we topped a hill. He wound down the window and shouted "*Vive la France!*" and his friend waved.

We left Oldtown along Leclerc Road. It's a name familiar to anyone who knows France because not only is Leclerc one of the country's main supermarket chains but it was Philippe Leclerc—no relation—the general at the head of the 2ème Division Blindée which liberated Paris in the war. Leclerc Road moved peacefully along the northern banks of the lake, narrower now where we had rejoined it but just as beautiful. Homes and fishing cabins lined its banks, bringing life but keeping themselves just the right distance apart to preserve the view. A lean man on a racing bike sizzled up beside us on narrow tires, his legs shaved, his red jersey tight to his body.

"Great day to be riding!" he smiled. His legs kept turning slow circles on his massive gear as he rode at our perfectly-fast-enough-thanks pace.

"Did we just see you going the other way?"

"Yeah, I work just down there…" He waved towards Usk, still unseen. "I get some riding in on my lunch break." We sensed his hour was nearly up, that every minute counted. "Well, you folks have a great day," he said and then he was away, out of the saddle, the pedals turning slowly and then faster and faster until he was a little red blip in the distance.

Usk is across the water from the tiny Kalispell reservation. It has an impressive tribal headquarters and, in the valley, a magnificent extended teepee that would be, in other circumstances, an excellent big-top for a circus. Signs pointed to the powwow grounds. Buffalo roamed in a field and a wooden roadside church had wood pews and Christian artifacts.

Léo Woodland

A board outside named supporters or perhaps benefactors, maybe a church council. They had names like Foxman and Wildbear.

Indian tribes are as different from each other as the nations of Europe. And sometimes as hostile to each other when it comes to borders and territory. We wanted to know more, to discover how different the tribes and their reservations see themselves now. Are they separated by blood and history? Or are they united by circumstance and tragedy? There is certainly a difference between reservations. The uniting factor on the first two we visited was a lack of hope and, we noticed, a great many dirty cars with cracked windshields and dented bodies.

A cyclist is the first to see that a car is no sign of a driver's soul. But when *all* signs change, something is up. Here, the cars were new and clean. The few houses we saw were simple and plainly painted but that is Indian style. That much we had already learned. Extravagant housing, it seems, is the white man's way. More important was the indefinable air of confidence, of a presence, a future, we hadn't sensed elsewhere. And it was—I hope this doesn't sound patronizing—pleasing.

Kettle Falls has a large, pale blue sign advertising itself as "1,640 people and one grouch." It too is pleasing but it smacks of the contrived. Eight people, with not a black face or an Indian among them, are shown happy and smiling. One is not. Well, maybe it's me, the grouch. The town gets fun out of it and picks a grouch each year to commemorate and then holds a parade. Yes, I'm beginning to realize I *am* a grouch. What harm can there be in fun?

Signs have been there since 1992, just before the town's centennial. One used to say "Home of the 1992 Miss America." It doesn't any longer: not the one we saw, anyway. I only know it was there because I read the town guide. You would think it remiss of me not to tell you more. So I looked. And I found something curious. It was that the 1992 Miss America was Carolyn Sapp, described as "the first Miss Hawaii to achieve the title." She is, I found, "an established leading motivational speaker, a charismatic entertainer and a product spokesperson [*sic*]." She probably also loves her mother and hopes to travel. But where's the connection with Kettle Falls? Maybe that's why the sign's no longer there. Who knows? Who cares?

Even the centennial is an odd date. The guide says settlement began in 1816, possibly a little later. The centennial seems to celebrate the point at which people realized that, yes, they had built a town. A writer back in 1901 remembered: "Where a few months before there was nothing but gloomy, sighing forests, in 1891 appeared a city! Pines, spruce, firs and tamaracks disappeared. In their places the most enterprising town in the western part of the United States made its magical appearance. Broad streets and avenues lined on either side by handsome business blocks, public buildings and princely residences sprung up to attract the attention of the entire state. There had been many boom towns in the west, especially in mining camps, which had spring up luxuriantly and acquired a large population in a remarkably short time. But there had never been anything in history to equal the spontaneity of this coltish town in the magnificence of its planning and the elaborateness of its buildings."

You can't see it now, though. It flooded in 1940 when the Grand Coulee Dam was built. Indians were less than amused because they lost their homelands, to which they had been banished by the government in the first place, and their burial grounds were moved. Some people went to the nearby Spokane and Colville reservations. In 1952 the tribes sued the government. They had been denied the "fair and honorable dealing" promised in their resettlement. The case dragged on and aspects fizzled out. But in 1992 a court awarded them $53 million and a percentage of the money the dam made for as long as the dam existed. Maybe *that* explains why the reservation appeared so much more prosperous.

There is a routine to all things. Our own, established over many tours, became more honed as we went. Most nights we camped. There were more motels than we would have chosen in the Adirondacks but that was because of the weather. We knew it would be chilly; we didn't know it was going to snow. After that we camped most nights and settled for a hotel if we were wet, exhausted or if the camp site—as at Havre—was out of town. We arrive and spend a luxurious amount of time finding level ground with reasonable grass. The tent is a Hilleberg Nallo 2, a green tunnel we have had for a decade. It's made in Estonia even though Hilleberg is in Sweden. Inside, a nice touch, is the name of the man who made it.

I take it off the rack above the back wheel and start to put it up. Steph goes for a shower. I unload my four bags without taking them off the bike. I carry both sleeping bags and the self-inflating mats that go beneath them. I also carry the cooking gear, which I unload next. Then I string up the elastic line which will serve as a Nepalese prayer flag as our dripping clothes hang from it. By then Steph is back from the shower. She takes my clothes as I shower. By the time I come out, she has washed them. I wring them out and we peg them to the line. Usually they dry. Sometimes not. Most modern cycling clothes dry when you put them on but we have a spare set anyway.

We cook on a single-jet gas burner, using bottles of blended propane and butane. It's simple and clean. The disadvantage is that the bottles are expensive, especially in Canada and the USA.

It's surprising how early you sleep when you're cycling. We have a light to find things but nothing by which we can read. I read an account of cycle-campers who preferred to pitch beside an RV rather than a car. People in RVs vanish as dusk falls and they can't be heard. Car campers, on the other hand, set up a table and chairs and light a fire—no American worth his name can see an open space without wanting to set fire to something—and they talk into the night. "Please," the tired campers begged when their neighbors persisted in talking, "it's 7:30—can't you see we're trying to sleep?"

The morning also has its routine. I am one of those irritating people who look forward to each morning and whistle within moments. I get up, I put on water for coffee and start organizing things for breakfast. After a while the tent starts to shake. Steph is stuffing sleeping bags into bags. Then comes the rhythmic hiss-hiss-hiss as she squeezes the air beds into their bags. And then, when the coffee is ready, she emerges. We are on the road around eight.

On the road now meant on the passes. We faced a succession, starting outside Kettle Falls with Sherman Pass. It gets to around 1,700 meters, the only thing, he said with a gay laugh, that separates Kettle Falls from Republic, 73 kilometers away. Of that, the climb takes 40 kilometers so obviously it can't be that steep. Twenty-five miles of properly steep road would land you on the moon. And sure enough, it wasn't hard. It starts lower than the climb to Logan Pass, the peak of Going to the Sun, but it doesn't get as high and it takes twice the time to get there.

For a couple of hours, sure enough, it was easy, a gentle valley, a stream chattering to itself on our left. "The hardest part of this climb looks like being boredom" was Steph's observation as our computers clicked up one meter of effortless climb after another. We were in a green corridor, a road that could never cause offense but which never allowed a view of anything either. The trees were thick on both sides. Trees, dry bleached soil, on and on.

But then came the last hour. It wasn't that steep but it was steeper and by then the damage of the lower slopes had been done. The day grew hot and we rode and we stopped in shadows when we could and then we rode on. It's not so much tiredness that discomforts on a climb like this: it's being locked into one position, like a spring poised to unwind but never given the chance. The joy of stopping can't be overestimated. It took a long time because it was a long way. At the top we got a picture of the sign announcing that we had reached the top, it being compulsory for cyclists to take snaps of themselves on tops of mountains, and we felt appropriately smug.

There is even a club, the *Club des Cent Cols*, for those who have ridden more than a hundred of them, some of which have to be higher than 2,000 meters. To have ridden *merely* a hundred passes is, by definition, the sign of a beginner. In the Pyrenees one fall we struggled to the top of a pass at 1,750 meters. And there, with tables with wine and food, were 150 cyclists who had reached the summit unseen before us. The *Club des Cent Cols* were meeting. And being who they are, they met on a mountain top.

I was vaguely cross when I got to the top of Sherman pass. I am impressively ratty sometimes. Up by the summit there is a layby, what Americans call an overlook. We stopped for an overlook, to admire where we had been and our strength and youthful resilience that had brought us there. We were joined by two motorcyclists. There is a lot in common between cyclists and motorcyclists even though there are obvious differences. There is the same love of the road, the same happiness not to be as others are, and often the same sense of humor. Being ratty, I wasn't going to have any of that.

The fatter motorcyclist (see the way I need to point that out?) wore a road-weary yellow T-shirt that strained to restrain him. He had leather riding pants and he had a red bandanna round his forehead. He and others had passed us in a small group minutes before we reached the top. The pass is an evident classic for motorcyclists and they go up and down in lines, like noisy black swans.

"Used to ride a hundred miles a day," the man said, referring to himself.

"Used to?" I asked.

He nodded.

"The world is full of people who *used* to," I chided uncharitably. There was something about him I didn't like. I sensed that two people on loaded bicycles took away from his own prestige of having gone by motorbike. It wouldn't have been the first time. In Minot—where the sex shop gives handsome discounts for airmen, incidentally—we were greeted at our motel by a man on a giant Honda who asked, as though we would have noticed, if we had seen him on the road an hour earlier. He said he was riding across America. We showed as much interest as that was likely to get, which meant that, yes, we were interested but we weren't impressed. It struck us that riding a motorcycle was more demanding than driving a car but that, in the end, how far you got was a product of how long you spent doing it. The achievement was the time to do it. Suddenly the man fell quiet and walked off.

"I think," Steph observed, "that he's gone all across America with people treating him like a hero. I think he felt suddenly outclassed."

Anyway, the other motorcyclist, a shorter man with a rat's nest of dark hair made sweaty by his helmet—Washington is the first state we've been in that insists motorcyclists wear a helmet—said: "You ride a hundred miles on that thing?"

His face suggested that reduced his prestige as well. He'd never considered cyclists went further than, well, further than where they vanished from his rearview mirror.

"Have done," I said. The answer was accurate but if he concluded that we'd done it on this trip then so much the better. The truth was that we had ridden *nearly* 100 miles on a couple of occasions, pushed by violent tail winds. Both men nodded without saying more and watched us ride off and down the other side of the pass.

Sherman is a Spanish climb and a French descent. If you have ridden in the Pyrenees, you'll know what I mean. The French side is always the shorter and steeper. Spain takes its climbs in the style of a sleepy donkey. But what had been green on the way up, and which westerly rain-bearing winds should have made still more verdant on the way down, turned instead to black because of forest fires. The earth became dryer, stonier, paler. In times past this was gold and silver country. Indians lived here, again because poor land was the best the government would give them. And when it suited white men to take it back, they did. And why did they? Because in 1896 prospectors called Tommy Ryan and Phil Creasor found gold. A lot of it lay beneath Indian homelands, but who cared about that?

Incursions grew more and more frequent and so did Indian complaints. The way the government looked at it was that it couldn't station enough troops to keep gold hunters off the land so they might as well give it to them. Towns and townships grew up everywhere and sometimes died as quickly. Republic, which still dresses as a Wild West town on orders of the mayor, went from nothing to twenty saloons, seven hotels, nine stores and a mine that dug 2,400,000 ounces of gold. All in four years. Republic survived when the gold ran out. Others didn't and ghost towns are their tombstones. And the Indians didn't get their land back.

Wauconda pass was another on which life grew one side but not the other. Sherman pass would have been greener on the way down had there not been so many fires. Wauconda was green going up; it wasn't going down. Instead, at the top we looked down on a brown countryside that was to stay with us all day. Where we had hoped for green meadows and sunbathing badgers, we fell instead into a near-desert.

There is nothing but a sign at the top of the pass. There is a village a good freewheel over the top but it is little more than a café. We sat beneath Clint Eastwood posters and ate ham and eggs. Two other cyclists walked in and sat in the neighboring bar. We prepared to talk to them as soon as we'd finished eating. Then the woman, a slight creature in black, walked right past our table on the way to the toilets. We looked up to catch her eye but she walked straight by. We looked up again as she walked back but the same thing happened.

Cyclists usually fall on each other to talk of the road ahead, to share help. Cyclists are visible. If they're not in Lycra, they will be the only folk in shorts or hangman tights. They are not easily missed. Not unless you want to miss them. We got a faint nod as we left, and three shared words when Steph went back to fill our bottles. But apart from that, nothing. It seems a shame. Cyclists are so much a brotherhood that they wave as they pass. They stop for each other when trouble strikes. This happens all over the world. Except in Belgium, where cycling is too serious, and in Washington. We were quickly discovering that Washington cyclists are the least sociable in America. And we felt more sorry for them than for ourselves.

The road from there dropped into a lot of slow, flat roads through scrub, dry earth and rocks. People came here because of gold. Three brothers found it in 1896 and within two years, like in Republic, there were saloons, crude hotels and a range of businesses. A stage coach pulled in twice a week and dropped off still more people with gold dust in their eyes. A population of 300 doesn't sound a lot but even now it would constitute a community worth mentioning out here in the dry earth. And then, suddenly, the gold was no more. The hopeful lost hope and moved on. Wauconda now is that café and little else.

John Pflug was a dreamer, too. His unfinished house stood further down the pass, back from the road on the right. John and his wife Anna came to America in 1900. Lord knows why out here except that land was probably cheap but Pflug dreamed of recreating a bit of Germany. He would build himself a German house in the hills. His ambition was greater than his wallet, though, so that starting in the summer of 1908 he took on no help and hauled timber from a sawmill 10 miles away. He loaded his horse-drawn wagon, drove it up the hill, unloaded it and nailed up a little more house. Over and over.

He never finished it. It stands abandoned in a small ravine, low grassy hills on three sides. It is fenced off. Pflug died in 1956 and his wife two weeks later. By then their dream had stood empty and blown by mountain winds for 35 years. Their eight surviving children—two more died in infancy—live elsewhere. The dark wooden walls have caved in sideways. Much of the roof has collapsed. The windows are blind and empty.

It's a sad story, don't you think? And it matched the countryside. We could have been on the fringes of the desert. The cliffs that stood back from the road were a tormented collection of scars, deep gashes and outcrops. Tons of broken rock, sloped at 45 degrees, lay at their feet where the ground had dried and lost its grip. Gone were the blue rambles of sweet pea which had given so much pleasure the rest of the week. In their place, gorse and, above all, endless gray-blue bushes of what looked like but didn't smell of dried lavender.

There were no villages, just collections of inexpensive houses, little better than shacks, and now and then perhaps six old trailers dusty and stained by life. They huddled at the end of a short dusty path. How people lived, we had no idea. There were no factories, even small ones, and no sign of serious farming. It was a mystery and it lasted all the way to Tonasket, a busy and prosperous town worried, to judge by signs, by being a sudden junction at the foot of a hill down which plunge truck drivers in a hurry.

Some level of affluence returned after that. The fields were cropped. Gardens outside houses were again watered with such enthusiasm on a hot afternoon—38 degrees—that anyone with a hand for carpentry would consider building an ark. Nobody waters gardens more enthusiastically than an American. But it was still desert fringe. Not Sahara, of course, but rock desert. Not what we had expected, but interesting.

The euphemism was: "You watch out on that back road, now—there are a lot of drunk drivers about." It meant: "Watch out: you're about to go through an Indian reservation." That's what the woman said in a store that had an antique fuel pump and a leafy shelter from which hung old bicycles. The reservation, in fact, seemed unremarkable: a lot of open land, scattered, shabby houses, people who waved as we passed. Omak was also on Indian land, although there was little sign of it that an outsider could read. But how much it was Indian land came to us when we stopped the night in the stampede grounds.

I put up the tent as Steph rode into town for groceries. It was a big site and crowded. It was no surprise to see people walk up and down the river that edged it, although the water and what lay behind were hidden by a bank of earth. I watched unsuspecting as half a dozen men rode by on horseback, some wearing padded jackets, some with helmets and others not. Lethargy and tiredness meant it was longer than it should have been before I stirred to see why the crowd on the bank was gasping.

They were gasping because the men I'd seen on horseback were rehearsing for the Omak Stampede in a week or two's time. The death plunge is its highlight. The rules are easily understood: 20 men on horseback line up at the top of a 75-degree earth bank that gets narrower as it gets lower. Someone shouts "Go!" and all 20 gallop— they don't just slide or canter or walk—to the bottom, barging each other as the funnel closes. They crash into the water with the effect of a destroyer fighting a storm and then struggle through the river and into the stadium on the other side. Simple as that. And terrifying.

"It's between the natives," a friendly woman holding a child said. "You never see a white guy do it."

I'm a white guy and I wouldn't do it. Downhill on a loaded bike can be thrilling enough. And a bike has brakes.

Here the rodeo racers of Omak were training alone or in pairs. On the day they'd race 20 at a time.

The guys I'd seen were practicing, and justifiably showing off as well, two or three at a time. They came out of the river without racing across it or into the arena, walked along the river bank, then took a bridge to the other side and disappeared behind housing. A handful of enthusiasts stood on the ridge and their excitement showed the horsemen were approaching. There could be 10 minutes between each spectacle. The riders edged up to the drop, to give themselves and the ponies a good look, turned, retreated, then with a lot of whooping took the plunge at a gallop. Occasionally a pony refused. Otherwise, impossible to read their minds of course, they seemed accustomed to what they were doing. The winner shrieked with joy when he disappeared in a fountain of white water and the loser stayed silent.

We didn't talk much, either, going up Loup Loup pass. It was hard. Very hard. It started on a ridge through bleached, dry countryside with not a tree to shelter us. We had moved from snow through the Adirondacks to uncommon heat through the Cascades. The road surface was slow and exhausting. There was no water. On the other side, however, were Twisp, named after the sound of a wasp and home of one of the inventors of the transistor, and then Winthrop. Loup Loup is the most disagreeable hill in America and Winthrop one of its most curious towns. One of its oddest aspects is that its first bar was opened by a man who detested alcohol. Guy Waring, a Harvard graduate, had this theory that running his own bar would keep out less discerning competition and he ran his place accordingly. As the town history says: "Anyone who started getting drunk was given the boot—a policy which must have greatly surprised many patrons."

Winthrop is a Disneyland of the Wild West, the work of a timber man called Otto Wagner. He came to town and founded the Wagner lumber mill. That made enough money that his wife Kathryn paid to turn the town into his memorial. If storekeepers turned their shop fronts into Wild West copies, she would pay half the price. Then the town would look as it had when her husband arrived. Not everybody was enthusiastic but other towns in the state had done the same and profited from the tourists who visited. Business was business and the conversion went ahead. They built wooden sidewalks, put false facades on buildings, erected hitching posts for horses that never came. The tourists came, though, and Winthrop sells them trinkets and Wild West "souvenirs." It's all fake, of course, but as quaintly fascinating as it was appalling. Not least the liniment advertisement, painted on a wall, of a man sharing his bed with a horse.

Léo Woodland

A thought occurred as we approached Washington Pass. If Sam had been described as both French and English, what were the chances that he was an Englishman living in France or a Frenchman living in England? There are a lot of both. So many French people live in London that, solely by its French population, it would be the eighth biggest city in France.

For the moment, though, our thoughts were more towards Canada. Tim was a Canadian. He was in our group when I first tried riding across America. There were a dozen of us, all unknown to each other except for a couple from Hawaii. It could have been a disaster. It was such a success that there have been reunions ever since. Just after this ride, I was due to host two weeks in France for everybody. Tim and his wife live in Revelstoke, in western Canada, just north of Winthrop. "Just north", of course, is a North American assessment. North Americans travel distances which Europeans would consider only with months of planning. To a European 100 miles is a long way. To a North American, 100 years is a long time. Tim and Jill rode down from Revelstoke on a yellow Honda with a yellow trailer. They looked as though they had been through a custard car-wash.

(A sign that the USA is a benighted country is that you can't buy custard in cans or condensed milk in tubes. There is a fortune for anyone who introduces either and all I ask is that you print my name in gratitude on the label.)

It was good to see them and it was even better that they managed to squeeze a couple of our panniers into their trailer. Washington Pass was our highest crossing in the Cascades, not hard in itself but daunting in the heat. The sun still beat enthusiastically in a state we had been told was wet and cold two thirds of the year. This was the wrong third, although we'd have complained even more in the rain.

We finally saw mountains worthy of the name. Until now they had been high but rarely impressive and sometimes they have been fairly ordinary. They had been hard—Loup Loup is evidence of that—but not until now did they stand high and arrogant, expressionless and contemptuous as we sweated to scale them. They reminded me of a Frenchman called Pellos who during the Tour de France of the 1950s and 1960s drew cartoons of smiling, avuncular mountains that held bags of loot just out of reach of riders. Or he showed men shredded and discarded from their cruel slopes. His mountains scowled and hid a monster who waited with a raised hammer to pound those arrogant enough to race their flanks.

Washington climbed less than Sherman Pass but the rocks were angrier and they were topped and streaked with long lines of snow, even in July. We climbed in 38 degrees, the sweat streaming but the road surface sweet. To climb in 38 degrees is not pleasant. And I, prone to the thinness of air above 1,500 meters, felt no better for that. In cooler weather it wouldn't have been half the problem. But we were shattered by the last hairpin that leads through rocks to the summit and grateful for the cold beers that Tim and Jill pulled from their trailer.

After that, Rainy Pass was just a hook in the road once it had started descending. It was another col sign for the collection but just a few miles' effort to justify it. And after Rainy Pass came 30 kilometers of descent. Whoopee! But more whoop than whoopee. Because the wind funneled between rocks and forced us to pedal as we descended. We didn't stop but we were down to the speed we'd have ridden on the flat. And the moment the road reached lower ground, it hooked back up. Several times. It was very debilitating. On the motorbike, Tim and Jill barely noticed. Nor did Jill notice Rainy Pass. And that is the difference between cycling and motorcycling.

Newhalem is a company town. If you didn't know that before you got there, you'd ask yourself questions once you did. There was a uniformity about the place, in the style of houses, in the lettering on signs. It's owned by the power company that supplies Seattle, and only company employees and those of that ilk can live there. For us it had three attractions. The first was a store, into which we spooned ourselves and ate and drank after a long, long time in the saddle. The second was an appealing steam locomotive parked on a green. And the third was the most beautiful camp ground of the ride, a sylvan glade with pitches set among trees. Birds settled unconcerned on branches and deer wandered within a few paces and stood and gazed with sad eyes before strolling on.

On the other hand, it's on sites like this that we most worried about poison ivy. We don't have poison ivy in Europe any more than we have dangerous weather and poisonous snakes. And when you know it could be there, and you're not at all sure that you'd remember, let alone recognize it, you get just a little paranoid.

Léo Woodland

I was warned about it by wiser hands on my first ride in America. At one point I rested my bike against a bush for the night only for Tim to announce with what I thought needless glee: "I think you've just put your bike in a load of poison ivy." For fellow Europeans, I must point out what all Americans know: that poison ivy is not at all like stinging nettles. Stinging nettles are as bad as it gets in Europe. They touch and they produce an itch and that's it. Poison ivy doesn't itch. Not at first. You find out only later that you've brushed against it. It contains an oil which works on your skin until, in the words of a song, "you're gonna need an ocean of calamine lotion." And because it's an oil, it can lie unseen on your bike and bite you when you next touch it.

The first time I heard of it was the mid-1960s. I bought a Rolling Stones EP—an Extended Play, somewhere between a 45rpm single and a 33rpm album, or long-player as it was known then—on which one of the songs was *Poison Ivy*. To many people it is a comedy number. But I've never known Mick Jagger to sing comedy numbers. So when he warned "She comes on like a rose, and everybody knows, you'll be scratching like a hound, every time Poison Ivy comes around," it wasn't likely he was singing about gardening. Venereal disease, yes, a good-time girl, yes, but not weeding and pruning.

Finding that poison ivy, without capitals, was a plant less devastating than syphilis was welcoming but not entirely comforting. And for three months we had worried about it. A couple of days remained now before we reached the Pacific. We hoped we would survive that long, especially given cyclists' habits of peeing in the bushes. Or "going to the bathroom in the woods," as I heard one American put it.

It was strange having the Rockies behind us. For so long, like the Mississippi, they had been a waypoint. The Rockies in particular, because in the end you just take a bridge across the Mississippi and that's it. A mountain range, on the other hand, you live with on the horizon for a week and you suffer for a week. And then, like a coughing fit, it's over. Now we had just the gentle Skagit valley, green and slightly sloping in our favor, spoiled by the power lines running from Newhalem. Keep your eyes low enough and they vanished but it achieved no more than a child who closes its eyes against a monster.

We stopped for coffee at a gas station in Marblemount. The village has three restaurants or cafés and they were all shut. The gas station had tables and chairs outside and a place to leave bikes. We went inside. The usual aisles of canned or sugary food ran the length of the place, with shelves on the wall behind them. I attended to the important things, like seeing where the coffee and Sticky Buns were, which left Steph time to look after the lesser jobs, like worrying what we were going to eat that night.

I had just returned to tell her I had found the coffee and to ask how she was getting on when a slim, lean man with an open, tanned face, brown eyes and short dark hair walked along the other side of a central aisle. That's all we saw of him, decapitated as he was by rows of Pringles.

"That's either a cyclist or a runner," I whispered.

Steph was quicker-thinking.

"Are you Sam?" she asked. I was astonished. It had never occurred to me.

He looked across, equally surprised.

"Are you the couple from Toulouse?" he asked back.

We had finally met Sam. And he had finally met us. Gary and Deb, whom we'd met back in Glasgow on July 4, had missed the loop through Cardston and passed Sam a week or so earlier. News of us had reached him from others who'd taken a more direct route to Anacortes and the Pacific. He had less news of us than we had of him, and less idea where we were, but news of our following him had intrigued him.

And was he British or was he French? The answer was yes, to both. Or at any rate, he was British but he had lived for years in Castillones, where he worked as a builder. There were two surprises there. The first is that his accent and elocution were not at all that you'd expect in a wheelbarrow operator. The second is that Castillones is only half a day's ride north of where we live, in southwest France. Toulouse is simply our nearest city and the only one worth mentioning this far from home.

"I used to live in Bristol," Sam enunciated.

"You don't speak with a Bristol accent either." Bristol, or old-time, working-class Bristol, is the accent you use to imitate a pirate.

"We lived in one of the posher areas," he smirked with an air of self-mockery.

He went to college, dropped out, went to France and started working. For the last three months he had been riding from Maine to the Pacific, inspired by a trip he made some years earlier but enjoying it less.

"Maybe that first time was a novelty," he said, "something different. It's not the same now. Too much seems the same."

Léo Woodland

Some of it, he agreed, was that he was riding alone. He was self-sufficient but several times we had word on the road that he was lonely, which means he must have mentioned it and therefore that he felt it quite badly. We had caught him with just a day and a half to go.

We took a back road from Marblemount, a tire-grabbing surface and a succession of hills, we on our road bikes and Sam on his mountain bike. We emerged in Rockport, having ridden the width of a continent to see the self-kicking machine. You may struggle to see the point of such a thing but it is of what America is made. That's why it was made. Because there was no point in making it. It took a genius to persevere, surrounded by gloomy doubters who lacked vision, to contrive a star of four spokes, each topped with boot. And then, that last step that distinguishes genius from the mundane, to make sure the only way to turn the wheel was to bend over in range of the spinning clogs. This was the stuff for which momentous journeys were made.

It stood, we knew, on the forecourt of a filling station. We saw a filling station the moment the back road reached the main highway. But the kicking machine wasn't there. Could there be another garage? Had the wheel been moved to a museum or a cultural center? We went to ask.

"Done for by the snow," said a middle-aged man filling a pickup large enough to supply an army division. "Stood right there." He pointed to marks on the floor of the forecourt. "Gone now, though. Went last winter."

"You know why it was there?"

"Somebody's wacky idea, I s'pose. But no, I never asked."

There was nothing to do but eat Sticky Buns, standing outside the garage, munching and reading the cardboard advertisements looking for baby-sitters. And then a more elaborate, colored post caught our attention. It had a fuzzy picture of a man who could have been in his fifties. He stood side-on, wearing a white shirt. He may have had a white goatee beard. It didn't need to be clearer because the tone suggested that everyone would know him. Underneath were the words: "Charlie Medford recently had a stroke. He is in Harborview and could really use some help paying his medical bills. Friends and Family of Charlie have set up a bank account for donations towards his medical bills. Any donations would be greatly appreciated. Thank You."

We were shocked. It was strange for Europeans, accustomed to health care from cradle to grave, to face the reality of life in the richest country in the world. America makes its priorities clear: the rich are lauded but the sick can be left to die. "There is a strange relationship between the system of a country and its people," said Quentin Crisp, the ultimate Yankophile, in *Resident Alien*. "In England, the people are hostile to a man but the system is compassionate. The very old, the very young and the ill-equipped-to-live will always be looked after. In America everyone is friendly—almost doggie-like—but the system is ruthless. Once you can be pronounced unproductive, you've had it. You will end up living in a cardboard box at the corner of a street where once you occupied a mansion."

What we didn't find to eat in Rockport we found on the concrete-surfaced Main Street in the subtly named town of Concrete. The story is that settlers came up the river in 1871 and called the west bank Minnehaha. The post office decided the name was silly and changed it to Baker. Those across the river worked for Washington Portland Cement and gave themselves the entirely unenigmatic name of Cement City. Baker resented that people with a duller name should have better jobs and in 1908 they welcomed the Superior Portland Cement company to their side. For a while both towns glared at each other across the water. And then they decided it would be better to merge. In 1909 they settled on the name Concrete. To make sure you don't miss it, it is written in huge capitals on a massive cement silo on the edge of town. CONCRETE, it says in red. No argument.

An enchanting history it's had, too. In 1912 it had the first phone service in eastern Skagit County, which admittedly isn't a huge geographical area but remains something of which the town is proud. Two sisters, Kate Glover and Nell Wheelock, built it. Nell climbed poles and strung lines and Kate ran the switchboard with their niece, Ethel. You made a call by cranking a lever on your phone. Kate or Ethel answered, plugged your line into someone else's and cranked again. If there was a reply, you started your conversation. If there wasn't Kate or Ethel promised to find them and get them to call back.

By April 16, 1931, the sisters had sold their little business to the Skagit Valley Telephone Company 30 miles down the river. They wouldn't have taken the call that two gunmen had entered State Bank on Main Street and taken $4,491. To discourage a shoot-out, the bandits bundled the bank's president, a clerk and a customer into their car and sped away. Or, at any rate, sped away as fast as a car will go with two bandits, three hostages and several sacks of money.

The alert started when locals saw dollar bills in front of the bank and no one inside. The policeman called for a roadblock and set off with a posse. The bandits grew tired of their hostages four miles west of town and abandoned them. They then drove to a farming community six miles east, went over a steep embankment and took a boat down the Skagit. They were never caught. Many years later a bear-hunting guide claimed to have been one of the bandits. He said he had lost all the money in "a crooked dice game" in Seattle but nobody knew whether to believe him.

More comical was the night Orson Welles broadcast War of the Worlds on the radio over Halloween. He moved the scene to the eastern USA and turned it into a seemingly live report which interrupted a dance-band show. A breathless reporter spoke of terrifying scenes in front of him. In New York and New Jersey, people panicked and fled town. Americans have an enthusiasm for being scared by unseen but threatening forces and that night Concrete was keener than most. The concrete plant's electricity station short-circuited with a flash and the town went dark at the point when Martians were invading with flashes of light and poison gas.

People fainted. Others grabbed their families to head into the mountains. A man was said to have run two miles to town in bare feet. Others grabbed their guns, and one businessman—a Catholic— pushed his wife into their car, drove to the nearest service station and demanded gas. Without paying, he rushed to Bellingham 45 miles away to see his priest for absolution. He told the gas-station attendant that paying "wouldn't make any difference—everyone is going to die!"

We have learned many things on this trip. We, Europeans largely ignorant of American history, discovered the Underground Railroad. We learned of railroad barons and Indian clearances. And now we learned about Lewis and Clark. Meriwether Lewis and the much less ambitiously named William Clark are huge in American history. We have followed much of the pair's northern route across America. We didn't know that before we set off but signs began telling us since soon after the birth of the Mississippi. There was even a bike route named after them. You'll know, of course, that Lewis was Thomas Jefferson's secretary at the White House and seemed an ideal government choice as a great explorer because he had barely been to school, knew barely anything about maps and plants and couldn't speak Indian languages. His violent mood swings suggested a mental disorder. Just the man to pick.

Not wanting to be intellectually outclassed, Lewis asked his pal William Clark to go with him. Clark had had even less schooling but, despite that or perhaps because of that, he was described as "steady and brave." Like Eisenhower crossing America with spotlights and breakdown crews a century later, Lewis and Clark set off up the Missouri in 1804 with 32 soldiers, 10 civilians, a slave, three interpreters including a teenage girl with her baby, and a dog. They spent two and a half years traveling 8,000 miles. When they got to the Pacific, the local Indians greeted them as "son-of-a-pitch", thinking that was how white men greeted each other. They also found an Indian woman with "Jonathan Bowman" tattooed on her leg. They weren't the first white men to pass that way.

Their diary, written with the orthographic liberty you'd expect, detailed 178 plants and 122 animals, including the grizzly bear, which they encountered. The nation was pleased and Clark was made governor of Missouri Territory and Lewis governor of Louisiana Territory. Lewis never did get over his mood swings and, only three years later he went crackers in Grinder's Tavern in Tennessee, talking to himself and acting so oddly that the innkeeper moved out. Lewis then blew out most of his brains.

Jefferson presumably read, or had a summary made, of their findings but after that they dropped into the unknown. It was only when a naturalist found their account in a closet in Philadelphia that their findings reached a wider world. A world which reveled in their bravery but despaired of their spelling. Of their passage through Wolf Point, for instance, Lewis wrote:

> Just opposite to the birnt hills there happened to be a herd of Elk on a thick willow bar... I determined to land and kill some of them accordingly we put too and I went out with Cruzatte only. we fired on the Elk I killed one and wounded another, we reloaded our guns and took differnet routs

through the thick willows in pursuit of the Elk; I was in the act of firing on the Elk a second time when a ball struck my left thye about an inch below my hip joint... the stroke was severe: I instantly supposed that Cruzatte had shot me in mistake for an Elk as I was dressed in brown leather and he cannot see very well; under this impression I called out to him damn you, you shot me, and looks towards the place from whence the ball had come... I do not believe that the fellow did it intentionally but after finding that he had shot me was anxious to conceal his knowledge of having done so.

It says a lot of their buccaneering approach to the journey that he went hunting with a man who couldn't see.

I mention all this because Lewis and Clark were excited to reach salt water—"Ocian in view! O! The Joy!"—and so were we. Well, it wasn't precisely the ocean, it's true. And it was too chilly for hula girls wearing little but a smile. It rained much of the morning and it never got much better. But riding gently down the slope through the village of Bay View, we saw the inlets of the Pacific for the first time. We had ridden 7,264 kilometers. From a distance the gray water was barely distinguishable from the sky. And then we reached the foot of Josh Wilson Road and we could smell the salt and the seaweed and the dull odor of wet mud.

We maneuvered our bikes through metal barriers set close to keep out motorcyclists—"but so close that there are a lot of Americans who couldn't *walk* through them," Steph said—and bumped idly along the Padilla Bay shore trail. It ran out over salt marshes and the mud and creeks of low tide. Seagulls flew and swirled, shouting at us, although there were fewer than I expected. White smoke or steam rose from a refinery across the water.

The path took a curve beside abandoned and rotten hulks of boats tied to decomposing posts by long strands of rope hung with seaweed. Mysterious distorted timbers rose from the saline mud like the grasping hands of a drowning giant. It wasn't the Pacific as I had imagined it but we were there nevertheless. All that remained to Anacortes was a stretch beside a busy highway, on a path maintained by the Skagit Bicycle Club. Streams of RVs passed on their way to the ferry to the San Juan islands across the bay.

Sticky Buns Across America

If you have ever read *Clochemerle*, about a small French village, you will know the first world war broke out because villagers couldn't decide where to build a lavatory. The row became so intense that the army was called in, and when events got still further out of hand they drew in national politicians who, having to attend to Clochemerle instead of trouble in Europe more widely, found themselves at war with Germany because they had missed an important meeting.

While it's true that stuffier historians attribute the war to other causes, there's no dispute that armies assembled, war threatened and Kaiser Wilhelm had to arbitrate because of a pig on the San Juan Islands. Within two months of the pig's eating potatoes that it shouldn't, five British warships with 70 guns and 2,140 men were ready to open fire on 461 Americans with 14 cannon.

At the root of it was Charlie Griffin's black pig. Griffin was British and his neighbor, Lyman Cutlar, was American. Cutlar took a walk round his garden on June 15, 1859, and found Griffin's pig digging up potatoes. Cutler was especially displeased because it wasn't the first time, so he lifted his gun and shot the pig. The two men understandably fell out.

"It was eating my potatoes," Cutlar protested. Griffin, entertainingly, was said to have replied: "Well, it's up to you to keep your potatoes out of my pig."

Cutlar didn't think this adequate or logical. He wanted to keep the peace, though, so he offered Griffin $10 to get another pig. Griffin said it wasn't enough, that he wanted ten times as much. Cutlar said no pig on earth, or at any rate on the San Juan Islands, was worth $100 and he refused to pay.

Griffin called on British police to arrest his neighbor. To him, the islands were British. The problem was that the treaty establishing the boundary wasn't clear, the result of which was that America considered them American. Americans who lived there could see their claim being squashed if the British enforced the law and they called on the American army to help. That irritated the British and three British warships turned up. America sent 66 soldiers of the 9th Infantry to fight them on the beaches. Both sides stared at each other, each ordered not to fire the first shot. Some relief came when a British admiral told to land marines said he wouldn't because "two great nations in a war over a squabble about a pig was foolish."

Léo Woodland

Washington and London were relieved. News traveled slowly and they were close to war before they even heard the improbable cause. Each country agreed to keep its army at opposite ends of the island. The soldiers found they got on well. They drank a lot together, making a point of celebrating each other's national holidays, and they held running races and other competitions. It quite suited them to be there more than a decade later, both nations still in a face-off over a pig. Sometimes things would flare up, as when local British commanders called for redcoats to take back the whole of Puget Sound. But other than that, the greatest threat to soldiers' lives was alcoholism.

After 12 years things started moving at fever pitch. The pig was referred for arbitration to Kaiser Wilhelm of Germany. I have no idea why. Nor did he, perhaps. He had never been asked to consider anything so grave and so he passed it on to a committee in Geneva. The committee met for nearly a year before siding with the United States.

War was averted. The only casualty was the pig.

The San Juan Islands were a distant thought as we crossed the long wooden trestle bridge that spans the bay to Anacortes. Two hundred feet of it had caught fire the previous fall. Ten years before that, the Tommy Thompson railroad stopped operating. So did Tommy Thompson, because he died, and the bridge was named after him. He'd spent 25 years building locomotives and rolling stock. Some of the track remains in the town. Eighteen inches wide, it is. For 13 years Tommy had driven his trains across 14 blocks of Anacortes, the cars made of polished cherry and brass, fitted with velvet cushions. The bike path through town is named after him.

At the end of the path, out where stunted ships stood like dead metal beasts in dry docks, our ride ended. Or this part, anyway. We had ridden from the sweet and salt water of the St. Lawrence river in Montreal to the purely saline water of Puget Sound, a continent and another language away. We spent a day in Anacortes and then another out on the ocean, watching orca play in the gray water in front of us. We saw Mount Olympia, snow-topped, across the inlet in Canada, knowing that soon we would be heading that way. For the moment we were going south to Seattle and then back north through Vancouver and around the Canadian Rockies. Another month. But I have taxed your patience too far. You have crossed North America with us, sometimes

I hope with the pleasure we felt but also, doubtless, occasionally with the boredom and even pain. If it was more of the first than the second, we are pleased and grateful; if it was more of the second, we can only apologize and promise better next time.

Please, sir, can I be a Geezer of Fury as well?

9 780985 963606